T0065755

FEASTING
THE HEART

BOOKS BY

REYNOLDS PRICE

REYNOLDS PRICE

FEASTING
THE HEART

FIFTY-TWO
COMMENTARIES
FOR THE AIR

A TOUCHSTONE BOOK
PUBLISHED BY SIMON & SCHUSTER
NEW YORK   LONDON   TORONTO   SYDNEY   SINGAPORE

TOUCHSTONE
Rockefeller Center
1230 Avenue of the Americas
New York, NY 10020

For information about special discounts for bulk purchases,
please contact Simon & Schuster Special Sales:
1-800-456-6798 or business@simonandschuster.com

Set in Electra

Manufactured in the United States of America

1   3   5   7   9   10   8   6   4   2

Library of Congress Cataloging-in-Publication Data is available.

ISBN 0-7432-0369-0
0-7432-0370-4 (Pbk)
ISBN 978-0-7432-0370-8
"AIDS House" by Lightning Brown, *Untouchable Clouds*,
St. Andrews College Press, page 39. Copyright © 1997
by the Estate of Lightning Brown. Permission granted by
Nancy C. Brown.

FOR

ADAM RUSSELL

CONTENTS

*Not broadcast.

FEASTING
THE HEART

PREFACE

In the fall of 1993, Alice Winkler of National Public Radio's "Morning Edition" asked me to write a short story for broadcast the coming Christmas morning. I don't recall that she gave me a word limit, but she did suggest that the reading time should not be longer than five minutes. Writing a cogent story that traces a narrative arc in so little time proved a hard assignment. Outside the Bible there are few such published stories, though the oral tale-tellers of a given tribe or family specialize in such miniatures.

I began by thinking of a quickly rounded story from my first Christmas away from home, I wrote it down as simply as I thought I could manage, I read it aloud with a stopwatch — way too long. I read it faster, to a tape machine, and heard myself gobbling inaudibly. I returned to work and sweated every conceivable atom of fat out of my prose — still too long. In some frustration, I phoned Alice Winkler and read her the story. She agreed to use it, as was. So I taped the thir-

teen hundred words at the local NPR station and went
to New Mexico for the holiday with friends.

While they were still sleeping on Christmas morning, I listened to my story on a palm-sized FM Walk-
man and thought how many more people were
hearing this lean narrative than had ever experienced
any other prose of mine. Maybe the thin high desert
air had me hyper-elated, but why not phone Alice
and propose a spot once a week from now on? In no
more than twenty years, say, I could read through my
accumulated life's work—once anyhow.

Such prospects could tempt a man down badly
wrong roads. But for better or worse, I well knew that
American radio—even Public Radio—has a very small
appetite for any prose that cannot be labeled, in some
sense, *news*. It's only Britons and Canadians who're
believed capable of sitting still for serial read-throughs
of novels, whole books of stories, or essays (despite
the fact that a great many taped novels are sold each
day for bedtime or travel-time listening).

So when, out of the blue, Margaret Low Smith of
NPR's "All Things Considered" contacted me in the
spring of 1995 and asked me to write and record sporadic
commentaries for that inventive show, I was surprised
and found myself accepting before I knew the details
of the job. The details proved simple. I'd be joining a
team of commentators that included such proven mas-
ters of the brief essay as Bailey White, with her perfectly
tooled parables from life in south Georgia, and Garri-
son Keillor, that virtuoso of post-Lutheran prose. Like

them, I'd be free—theoretically—to write about anything I chose, so long as I didn't violate federal or state statutes or the laws of common decency. The tenor of any given piece could be narrative, critical, nostalgic, comical—whatever, so long as it was clearly concise and at least temporarily interesting.

For, again, concision was the prime virtue. Any taped piece more than four minutes long might wait a good while before finding a sufficient hole in the day's rushing news. For each piece aired, I'd receive a sum of money that would buy dinner for two at a modest good restaurant. I braced myself with the thought that I'd grown up in a storytelling culture which dreaded boredom—the American South—and then I plunged into the likable procedure.

In brief, whenever I thought of a commentary, I'd write a draft and e-mail it to Margaret Low Smith in Washington. She'd phone me back, I'd read it aloud to her, we'd edit for clarity and speed. Then Tom Wilson, an affably excellent soundman from Duke University, would come out and tape the piece—often more than one at a time (they tend to come in batches). We'd ship them north to Margaret, she'd write one-sentence introductions and closings; and they'd wait on her shelf for some evening when the news yawned sufficiently to permit my thoughts.

Thoughts are what they've generally turned out to be, as opposed to narrative scenes or ringing demands; and I built my own set of thinking rules in the first few months. Be sufficiently serious, unless you intend an

occasional comic fantasy like "The Mad Inventor";
don't be a common scold or yet another long-wattled
media curmudgeon; but do permit yourself chances to
grow even more serious when the subject requires, as
in "My Tolerance Problem." Employ whatever in the
internal or external world offers itself as likely, sup-
pressing only the identities of shy friends or of enemies
whom I feel no need to excoriate by name. Finally, be
vigilant of the fact that even the briefest stretch of verbal communication—a phrase, a sentence—can be
wearisome; and boredom is again the state I've hoped
to avoid more strictly than any other except deceit.

The commentaries began to be aired on the late
afternoon of July 28th 1995, and they continue into the
new century. Gathered here are the first fifty-two—
counting the Roman Christmas story, which is a narrative essay. The two pieces indicated by asterisks in the
Table of Contents and in the text have not been broadcast; but I include them by way of owning up to the
kinds of subjects on which Margaret, an editor of
superb eye and instinct, felt I ran below par or beyond
the interests of our audience.

With a single exception—the last—the pieces
appear in the order in which they were aired; and
that's very nearly the order of composition. The unused
pieces are likewise set in the order of their arrival. In
general, with all the others, the text is the broadcast
text. Occasionally I've restored passages trimmed in
the interest of pace, and a few times I've added a sentence of clarification or an illustrative image. I've even

retained a few repetitions of thought and language. Some of them were necessitated by their contexts, though some are frankly the results of a failure to recall what I'd said before.

Commentaries is NPR's word for my pieces and for all the others in their long series. I might argue that *commentary* is a more ponderous word than my own efforts require—think of all the massive theological and political commentaries of the past. My pieces are at least as much essays. Our English word *essay* derives from the Old French word for *trial* or *attempt*. Accordingly, these fifty-two pieces are swift attempts at doing what fiction or poetry or philosophical comment can almost never do—reach a listener, a reader, instantly.

What he or she cannot retain and parse as your talking voice flees past him is finally useless—an unnerving equivalent of the tree that falls, mute, when the forest is empty. So five years of intermittent work at these attempts has been good exercise in utter concision and simultaneous clarity, qualities that have not always come naturally for me, even in the early days of schooling.

In fact, I've often felt (while trimming the excess syllables from a phrase or dispelling an obscurity) that I'd sent myself back to school—the old school of elementary composition where, facing the dorm clock at four in the morning, you confront the inevitability of a nine A.M. class assignment: Monday morning's five-hundred-word theme. What do I know that's interesting enough but not too interesting, and how can I say

it between now and daybreak in a clean two pages?
Where to start, how to stroll along for a paragraph or
two, how to end? I was a boy who relished school—it
seemed to be all I was good at—but I'd lost the scholas-
tic sensation years ago.

And that's despite the fact that life turns out to be
school every inch of the way, even in those long autum-
nal stretches when we convince ourselves that we've
graduated and will never again be tested. One unfore-
seen reward of the five years' work has been a sense of
almost literal sinew growing in my hands—I find
myself trying to trim all prose, however compact, to the
barest bone: my own, the Gettysburg Address, the Pre-
amble to the Constitution, even the Lord's Prayer.
I've yet to tell my friends, but the fascination with
sinew often has me silently editing their talk as it
emerges; and when I see occasional transcriptions of my
own talk, I cringe at the verbiage. One of President
Eisenhower's famed syntactically surreal press-con-
ference replies seems laconic by contrast.

Another welcome result of these particular attempts
has been the rapid e-mail response they evoke, the
mostly sane letters and the voices of strangers in public places, saying they've heard one and when's the
next due? I almost never know their air dates, which is
why I relish all the more the story of a certain woman
of extraordinary skills who—once she's heard, from her
local announcer, that one's on the way—steps out to
her car where the radio's better and listens from there.

Thanks then to her. A deep bow to Margaret Low Smith, to Alice Winkler; to Ellen Weiss and Darcy Bacon, my new producers; to Tom Wilson, to Susan Moldow, and a few million ears.

A CHRISTMAS IN ROME

I was twenty-two years old and still hadn't spent a Christmas away from home and family. That day though I was half laid back in unmarred sun on a bench in the one true Colosseum — Italy, Rome, December 25th 1955. Europe had only begun to believe that the devastation of Hitler's war might be survived, and even in Rome the sight of a winter tourist was rare as a failure of courtesy.

I'd left my room and made my way down through the city past ruins posing in vain for their picture — today they were empty of all but cats and ghosts of assorted psychotic Caesars, woolly Vandals and Visigoths. I'd even walked the length of the Forum and on across to the Colosseum with no sure glimpse of anybody as lost and foreign to the place as I and not a sign of holly and gifts.

I'd passed a few couples, sporting that brand of Italian child who easily seems the world's most loved; and some of the parents had bowed at my greeting. But the Colosseum was likewise empty of all but me and one of the bent old ladies who then sold tickets to everything Roman, toilets included.

So there, lone as Robinson Crusoe, I had one question—was I *lonely* in this grand place on such a high love-feast? It seemed the right question for a journeyman writer. I shut my eyes to the broad arena that drank the blood of so many thousands and let the Mediterranean sun burn its health deep into my bones.

The answer was No. I was happy. I'd got the gene from both my parents; and despite a normally bleak adolescence, had been sheepishly happy most of my days—*sheepish* because I wondered still if smiles were the kit for an artist's life. Even if I was here today on one of the world's great magnets alone, I knew I was backed with a travel grant; my first short stories were down on paper; more ideas were ticking in me; and— best—in only three more weeks I'd join my first requited love who was skiing in Austria.

What but love had I ever wanted more than the freedom I tasted now? So I sat for the better part of an hour in those two lights—the sun and the fierce shine that leaked from my triumph. I was already well down the road to my work and my free choice of love. If another human being entered the Colosseum with me, I failed to see. So the place itself, for all its gore, conspired to keep my joy pure as radium, fueling my life with dangerous rays.

High as I was, I managed to nod awhile; and when

I woke a half hour later, I knew the sound of a distant bell had brought me back; its toll had triggered the chill I felt. The light in the midst of the arena was dimming; and my mind spoke out, strong as the bell — *What are you up to this far from home on this day, of all days, and lonesome as any hawk on a thermal? What can you learn here that you don't already know in your bones? Get the hell on home.*

If I'd seen or heard in the next two minutes the least reminder of the day at home — an indoor tree, some merciful laughter — I might have hailed the nearest cab and tried to board a westbound plane. But the guts of the Colosseum dimmed further till all I saw was purple murk — the locker rooms of gladiators, holding pens for the beasts and martyrs. And I knew I needed this strange lone time in whole new worlds; so when I stood to enter the day, I turned — not due north back to my room but south toward the Circus Maximus, flat on a plain below the devastated mansions of the Palatine Hill.

The film *Ben-Hur* with its chariot race was still four years ahead in time; but my high-school Latin book had showed the racecourse at its clamorous pitch — the oval track, the island round which the horses had turned, the ranks of the seats. I stepped across one strand of wire and walked to where the island had stood — no visible remnant of marble or horseflesh, brawn or fury. The ground was littered with modern paper, though there were signs of recent digging — the earth was freshly turned and spongy.

Again no other human in sight. By now I was well
into midafternoon. Surely Christmas mass was over;
shouldn't some of the family meals be ending? What
was the local Christmas schedule? Dinner at my pen-
sione was not till eight and would feature salt fish.
Even the beggars who walked the streets as late as
midnight were under cover, real shepherds from the
country who'd brought real lambs and homemade
bagpipes with weird music more Arab than Western —
a firm recall of the shepherds' role in the birth at the
heart of this darkest month.

It wasn't all self-pity then when I thought *I'm the one
lone man in Rome for the birth that turns the wheel of
the year.* I'd better aim back toward my room. I would
write this day down anyhow and save some piece of an
hour that suddenly threatened to down me. At the
third step, my foot stubbed hard.

I leaned and dug up a piece of marble the size of
my palm with a perfect vine leaf carved on its edge,
plainly ancient. I looked around me — still nobody, a
few fast cars half a block beyond. I hid the marble
deep in my pocket and walked ahead, my first real
robbery. Before I'd gone another ten steps, I drowned
the guilt by thinking *It's all you'll get today, ace.*

That was only the truth; and I'd got near the rim of
the Circus before I saw two people blocking my path.
Before I halfway understood, my first thought was
Well, Christmas in jail; and I froze in place. But then
I took the presence in.

A young woman maybe my age in a tan dress, a

coarse brown shawl on her hair and shoulders, one hand on the child beside her—a boy with filthy knees and a coat so tattered it hung in comical strips. Was he five years old or older and stunted? They were beggars surely but—no—their hands didn't reach out toward me, though their black eyes never flinched from my face.

I knew I had a handful of change, the feather-weight coins worth almost nothing; and I dug in another pocket to find them.

Before I'd brought them to daylight though, the woman shook her head once—No. She gave the boy a gentle push forward.

He came to me, solemn but sure; and when he stopped two yards away, he held his hand out clenched as if he offered a game.

I asked what he had.

He thought a moment, opened his fist and brought it toward me—a dark disk, half-dollar size, that was meant to look old.

They were selling souvenirs, likely fakes. I smiled a "No, *grazie*," holding both my hands out empty.

But the boy reached up and laid the coin in my right palm.

I'd spent hours with a boyhood coin box; and when I turned the bronze coin over, I knew it was real with the profile of one of the saner Caesars, Hadrian—worth maybe fifteen dollars. I still didn't need it and offered it back.

But the child wasn't selling. He returned and trotted to join his mother, never facing me and not returning to take the marble vine leaf I offered.

His mother's voice though gave me the first real news of the day. She stooped to the ground and scratched in the dirt to show where they'd just found the coin; then she launched a smile of amazing light and said what amounted to "You, for you."

I have it still, a useful gift.

1993

BOOK TOUR

I've been on the road with other books of mine in the past, so I might have anticipated the kind of response I'd get this spring as I followed the customary tour rounds of readings and signings. The whole way, though, I've been quietly struck, time and again, by brief close meetings with men and women who've borne the full blast of AIDS in their lives and who come or call in to radio talk shows to tell their own stories to me and whomever.

In more than six weeks, I've yet to give a reading at which at least one stranger hasn't come up with a copy of my book *The Promise of Rest*, asked me to sign it for some young man; then said "He'd wanted to be here tonight, but he's just too ill." I've likewise watched a man brought in by two friends who literally supported him on each side. He looked sixty years old but may have been forty, weighing under a hundred pounds with enormous blue eyes burning in a skull that was barely covered by transparent skin. At the end of my reading, he slowly rose in the back row of seats, nodded his head in my direction with a smile that must have exhausted his strength; then he turned and let his friends lift him out — no other word of message or question.

I've talked with a wife who nursed her husband through a slow AIDS death; with a sister who finally overcame her fear that, if she visited her dying brother, she might bring AIDS back home to her infant. I've recalled more than once an elderly woman, strong as an iron bar, who said that she'd told her dying son about a radiant near-death encounter she'd experienced in her own past. After that, he'd ask her often for the story, taking some comfort in her glimpse of light and rest; she told him about it right on to his end.

A few of these self-effacing heroes have read my novel; most have not; yet they all say somehow "Tell everybody you know 'This must stop.' This is no kind of shame, but it can't go on; this is too hard to take." Their eyes confirm an ancient refrain, renewed among us for the first time since the last of the great youth-killing plagues subsided forty years ago — *The saddest sight is your own child's death. They were meant to nurse you; not this wrong way round.*

And as I push on, airport to airport — Washington, New York, Atlanta, San Francisco, Denver, Minneapolis, Iowa City, Chicago, and home to Raleigh-Durham–Chapel Hill, the faces still come, each burned by a sadness almost past words, each saying to me (as though I would prove a mouthpiece to the

world) that what they and their lost kinsman have suffered is no shame at all. When they ask me to write a
few words in a book, what I most want to tell them is
that, far from a shame, their kinsman's patience and
their own selfless ongoing devotion are the only
glimpses of light in the depth of this unrelieved dark.

1995

THE LAST GREAT WEEPER

Among my friends I'm often called "the last of the truly great weepers." My mother, who was brave as a bear, would dissolve into quiet tears at moments of grief. My father, a man with genuine woes, wept once in my presence; but that was a striking moment for me at age five. I've inherited tears from him more than her.

On a December day in 1938, he'd taken us to a railroad siding in Sanford, North Carolina to catch a twenty-second glimpse of President Franklin Roosevelt descending from a train. As FDR paused atop his ramp for a big-shouldered wave, I was watching Father. Down his red cheeks, tears were pouring as the President stalked on his steel braces to a waiting car. Father knew that his life had been saved, in the pit of the Depression, by this damaged man; he was also tasting the visible proof of the President's exuberant refusal of pain and defeat.

So tears, from the midst of a joyful moment, started

early for me. I remember silent tears in grade school—
when the roomful of children sang a Christmas carol,
say, or after a hard-fought spelling bee. I was always
inventing explanations. I mostly claimed it was wind
in my eyes, though my classmates knew we were
locked indoors.

By the time I reached college, I was more in control but was gratified to note that my best teachers
wept unashamedly in front of their classes. One wept
as he read us Walter Raleigh's letter from the night
before his beheading; another as he read Matthew
Arnold's elegy for his friend Arthur Clough; the third
as he bade us goodbye (we'd been his first honors sem-
inar in History and were graduating).

In middle life I continued in seemly public control,
though I remember private tears connected with
romantic shipwreck or the deaths of loved ones. When
I confronted spinal cancer and paraplegia in my early
fifties, I recall a single resort to tears—behind a door,
in the wake of the baldly delivered diagnosis. But in
three more years of ordeal, my eyes stayed dry as the
hide of a self-respecting rattlesnake.

Lately, though, I'm misting over again. Talking
calmly with a friend or listening to a student, I feel my
lids brimming; and the question is whether to admit
the presence of tears and wipe them or to let them roll
like a banner of what the eighteenth century called "a
man of sensibility." Or as more than one friend has told
me "like a sensitive plant."

The question is why tears have recurred. I've been

healthy for years; my writing and teaching reward me well; and I live with a bumper harvest of friends, though like most people past midlife, I go to more funerals than I'd planned (there I only weep with the music). What's at work then?

Not sadness, I've decided. And I learned it last week when I saw the film *Apollo 13*, a story of tragedy averted by the stamina of American astronauts and engineers. I'd followed the actual story intently; but watching its well-made reenactment, as three young men guide a flimsy craft earthward with an excellent chance of roasting to cinders, I felt both suspense and the welling up again of tears. Only after their rescue, when lights came on in the theater round me and strangers gawked at my streaked face, did I understand (I'm a slow learner, nearly thirty years older than my father the day he wept).

Roman Virgil speaks of the *lacrimae rerum*, "the tears of things." What I've now understood is the fact that the tears I find in things are native to a primal hope of our species — to see our kind at the highest pitch of skill and luck — a flawless dive from Greg Louganis, a perfect A above middle C from Leontyne Price, a lost child found unharmed by searchers: those moments when somebody gets something *right*. Exactly *right*, the rarest event.

1995

BIRTHPLACE

I'm bound to be one of the last white middle-class Americans born in an actual home. In February 1933 my mother, for reasons I never thought to ask about till she was dead, chose to bear me in her family home — it was her birthplace, her brothers' and sisters' and two of her nephews', in the village of Macon, North Carolina. I was the eleventh child born in the house; I'm the last one left alive. So I feel not only relief in the rare times I see the place now; but as its only surviving product, I also feel some caretaking duty.

Yet since the one-story rambling white house passed out of my family's possession more than ten years ago, the only care I can offer it is mental, psychic. I can write about it, which I have — at length. I can visit it once or twice a year, passing it slowly on my way to the family graves up the road. That way, you pass the Baptist Church tennis court, where till just recently a polite sign requested that all players

"conduct themselves in a Christ-like manner"—I'm
still attempting to guess how Christ played tennis.

The house, which is known as the Rodwell-Drake
house, is more than a hundred and ten years old. But
it s in sturdy health today, needing only a coat of paint
and the shutters restored. Better still, it goes on housing a family—a growing family: red and yellow toys lie
waiting all through the wide yard. The children's parents have come this far north from Mexico to work the
pale green fields of tobacco—our decade's demon
plant. Even twenty years back, the shoulder-high stalks
and furry leaves of bright-leaf tobacco were the pride
of this whole end of the world and its main support.
The health of the crop was the subject of constant talk
hereabouts from early spring till late in the fall.
Tobacco was, quite literally, the resource that paid for
much of my childhood; saw me through college, and
sent me to England for graduate school.

Despite what we've learned of its dangers, tobacco
still funds the life in my birthplace, though these beautiful black-haired children, playing where I played six
decades ago, are as surely oblivious as I was then to the
undergirding net that bears them up through the hot
air—their father's labor in the scalding fields. From my
van I can hear the children's laughter and snatches of
the calls they throw one another—mainly in Spanish,
a language my mother and her father (Jack Rodwell,
who built the house) would have heard as stranger
than words from a creature borne down on a sun-
beam and pausing to ask for water or shade.

When the children halt beneath the great oaks and look my way with huge dark eyes, I also lack their language and can only wave—a smiling greeting. They pause in their laughter, returning my wave with solemn self-possession. Only when I've driven on do I wonder what single thing I'd have tried to say, if we shared enough words. Though I miss at least two of the dead from this house, like limbs of my own, and though I know a good deal about the hard pain my kin endured in these walls, any sentence I'd offer these children would certainly start with plain thanks that they're here in their vigor, fueled by the hope to thrive and last, in a house that would be in ruins without them.

They'd understand that no more than I would have, had some white-haired man paused in the road near my childhood home and offered me words from as far off as Mars—or in the chattering language of birds—however grinning and grateful-eyed he tried to be.

So I move ahead toward the graves of my kin; they welcome all visits.

1995

JAMES DEAN, STILL HERE

On the sweltering afternoon of September 30th 1955, the SS *United States*—swiftest of the grand last generation of Atlantic liners—was towed from its berth in New York Harbor and aimed toward England. I was twenty-two years old, poised at the rail in a blue seersucker suit and white-buck shoes. Near me stood thirty more American males, all my age and as innocent as I.

We'd graduated from college three months earlier, had won scholarships to study at Oxford University, and were bound toward a Europe we knew of only from black-and-white newsreels of World War II. Whatever *cool* we tried to muster, as salt air met our seamless faces and we broached the first swells, we were all as raw as any son of the prairies in a Henry James novel, borne toward "perfidious Albion" and the rotting palazzi of Venice and Rome.

Blank-faced and bushed, as the Statue of Liberty sank behind us, we stumbled to our triple-bunked cabins to spruce up. The owners had given us a break on tickets—second-class cabins at third-class rates. After quick naps, showers, and shaves, we trooped in our best toward the glaring white dining room. Our "best," in those pre-slacker days, involved immaculate creasing on our trousers, shoulder pads in our jackets, spit shines on our shoes, Windsor knots in our ties, and hair manhandled by serious chemical restrainers. We were shuffled in pairs among the circular tables—speechless doctors and their voluble wives, world-weary Washington secretaries, and the odd solitary posing as a wounded vampire or spy. The food was lavish, if hardly distinguished (I'd grown up with splendid Southern cooks); and my memory of the meal awards a lone star—the sailing-night dessert was a tub-sized Baked Alaska, my first encounter with that absurd confection.

Then up onto deck for a starlit stroll—my first chance to taste the day's big reality: I was On My Own for the first full time and would be on my own for three years to come. My boyhood home, my beloved but normally entangling family, were slipping behind me with every thrust of the ship's huge pistons. Already elated in the bracing wind, I joined a laughing squad of new friends and—a little warily—went to the bar (I'd come from a deep line of male alcoholics).

It happened just then. Three thousand miles west, north of Los Angeles, a silver Porsche brakes to avoid a turning car but the cars collide. The Porsche is shredded, its driver killed in the crushing instant. At the moment, no doubt, other humans are killed in the

country I've left; but that ruined Porsche holds the
corpse of a man barely older than I and immensely
gifted.

I'd encountered his work, in his first motion picture,
a few months past—*East of Eden*—and was stunned
by the power with which his small frame embodied a
central theme of male life: the ceaseless hunt for a worthy father (my own gentle and burdened father had
died the previous year; I was already hunting him in
my fiction). I didn't know, that first night at sea, how
the young man had finished two more films which
would earn him the lasting magnetism he shares with
Marilyn Monroe alone. Oblivious and happy well past
midnight, I climbed to my bunk.

Near dawn next day I heard something slide beneath the cabin door, the ship's newspaper largely
devoted to shuffleboard tournaments and dance con-
tests. On the front however, my eye caught a head-
line—"Actor James Dean Killed in Wreck." Feeling
I'd lost an actual brother, I stood in the chill air near
my sleeping friends and tasted again my heady freedom, the start of my work. I also guessed that James
Dean, though tragically stopped, would rush unde-
terred toward global fame.

All but impossible now to believe that his power-
fully searching face and body have been in a plain
Indiana grave these forty years.

1995

THE GHOST-WRITER
IN THE CELLAR

The novelist Graham Greene said that, if he reached an impasse in writing a story, he'd read the troublesome passage just before bed. Then he'd rise in the morning to find that, almost invariably, "the ghost-writer in the cellar" had solved the problem while he slept. Most writers I know have similar strategies for passive reliance on their mind's dark compartments. So do most people whose work flows primarily from their minds—physicists and mathematicians, architects and choreographers, even (I'm sure) great fireworks artists and the CIA's most uncanny code-busters.

Yet the vast resource of our unconscious mind and the techniques for tapping its wellsprings are almost never taught to students in any discipline known to me. In my own case—in the early 1960s, as a fiction writer ten years after college—I was still stumbling in

the thickets of puzzlement: why could I write fluently
on certain days, then go appallingly dry for weeks?

For a start, not one of my excellent teachers had so
much as mentioned the urgency of learning two
things:

—*first*, that creative thought (whether it concerns a lyric poem or the plan for an armchair)
is conceived in the human mind below the level
of our awareness and,
—*second*, that the mind resides in an organ called
the brain, which is (like all our organs) a piece of
meat with its own rules and needs of nutrition and
rest, stimulus and respect.

I was well into my thirties before I began to understand that my unconscious mind would—to an amazing extent—compose and deliver my novels, poems,
plays, and essays *if* I bothered to give it sane amounts
of good food and sleep, sane chemical and emotional
nourishment, and then made myself available—six
mornings a week—at a quiet desk with the phone
turned off and all distractions, short of falling meteors,
canceled for the hours it took me to transcribe my
mind's ongoing work. It has hardly failed me since,
though I grant that a reader who dislikes my work may
feel I take dictation from a fool.

Whatever's in me, I've used it steadily for more
than a decade; and—now that I'm back from a cross-
country book tour, have mailed off my next manu-

script, and won't teach again till early winter—I'm giving my mind the rest it needs. Since I'm lucky enough to have an assistant who does chores for me, the relaxation can be as total as fate permits—eight-hour nights, mornings of reading, an afternoon nap, evenings with close friends, the occasional movie or weekend trip. A great deal, in short, of what many hard workers would call *hanging out,* even *slacking off.*

I'd accept those descriptions, though I might amend them to *hanging around.* My bet, my risk, is that what I'm doing is quietly hanging my resting body round a deep spring-fed lake that, since it has proved so trusty in the past, may now be renewing itself beyond my reach. The main hope of course is that soon I'll catch sight of some craft rising, breaking the surface with its own strange fittings and a crew of imagined hands as real as my friends and enemies—a craft I can manage to board and steer.

That's the hope of crowds of others clearly—among them, the men who conceive the world's bridges; the women whose bodies are building infants in the silent dark; the children whose literal nighttime dreams will fuel whole lives of brilliant generosity.

1995

ORAL HISTORY

My genetic survivors will be my two nieces, grown now into admirable women. Luckily for me, they live nearby; and though we're all mired to the axles in our desperately urgent little lives, we manage to meet three or four times a year for a big dinner, braced with helpings of the family's oral history.

I share most people's dread of *other* people's family stories—nothing, except other people's accounts of their dreams, can be more numbing than recited fragments from the sacred narratives of others. But I dive at once into any chance at a skillful recounting of the grandeurs of my own kin's past. Not that my and my brother's forebears were giants of physical or mental prowess. They were middle-class artisans, clerks, mothers, spinsters in a rural county in the upper South. In books I've worked to record their ardent hunt for pleasure, life, and more *time*. My written versions of their existence constitute what feels to me like a saga with as bony a thrust as any tale of Icelandic battlers.

But the oral tales that survive in our family are generally comic, and their mythic vitality lies almost entirely in their laughter — laughter being the strongest sign of a will to endure. Admittedly we tell a few sad stories — the saintly aunt who may have attempted suicide in the midst of melancholia, my father's maiden aunt who was always said to stutter because "she'd been bit by a spider in her cradle." We even acknowledge the loaded fact that our Grandfather Price (born in 1861) died in 1929 while hallucinating an imminent bloody slave rebellion, though official slavery had ended more than sixty years back.

That same Grandfather Edward C. Price, whom none of us knew, stands at the core of more than his share of the untarnished stories. There's the one about the night he dressed for bed in the dark and was found hours later, snoring away in a satin nightgown that a visiting cousin had left in his closet — *pink*, with a large silk rose at the neck. There's the one about the night when he and Grandmother, both in old age, knelt by their bed for prayers. Christmas visitors had kept them awake till late, and quickly they fell asleep on their knees. When Grandfather woke in the dark — long hours later, freezing in his nightshirt — he made his creaking way to Grandmother, who was kneeling still, and shook her arm hard: "Lula, wake up, woman! *Damned* if we haven't been praying all night."

My brother and I have honed such moments to their likable bones, with gestures and rhythms that regale our kin at least. But the single story of Grandfather Price that interests me most comes from his boyhood. All his contemporaries called him *Cupe*, which was short for *Cupid*. And a hundred and twenty–odd years ago, Cupe Price and some other boys drove a buggy deep into the county in search of an abandoned gold mine. It was strange terrain; but the boys were relishing their ride, when the horse brought them suddenly to the edge of a cliff above a barren plain. Cupe Price is said to have leapt to his feet with feverish eyes, pointed wildly to the far horizon, and cried "The sea—boys, oh, look, the *sea!*"

No more than that. But it was decades after his death before we learned that the cliff where Cupe Price imagined "the sea" was in fact the dry shore of an ancient ocean, long-since receded. That's the one surviving tale of Grandfather which adds an instant of youthful ardor to the just nightmare of his final bed. So while the story expects no laughter, we go on telling it to honor the wonder of a kinsman's vision— a boy in about, oh, 1880, catching the only glimpse of the ocean he'd ever get, though the water he saw in blazing joy had vanished eastward eons ago.

1995

A HOLE
IN THE EARTH

When I was ill with spinal cancer eleven years ago, friends and strangers sent me herbal remedies, holy pictures, tracts to read, and tapes to hear. Grateful as I was for the concern, I found little help in the gifts (though I especially enjoyed one letter in which a woman assured me that she had "a whole convent of nuns praying" for me and that they "get results").

One suggestion, from hundreds, did snag in my mind. Had I thought of making a trip to Lourdes, the healing spring in southern France which marks the site of appearances by the Virgin Mary to a peasant girl in 1858? Since watching Jennifer Jones's incandescent performance in *The Song of Bernadette* in 1943, I'd been curious about that girl—Bernadette Soubirous. And I knew that the writer Flannery O'Connor had journeyed to Lourdes toward the end of her killing battle with lupus. But a risky journey to such a com-

plicated place was past imagining in my hard times.
And as my recovery slowly surfaced, though I was
paraplegic and required a full-time wheelchair, the
thought of a pilgrimage faded entirely.

Still, before and since that crisis, I've discovered
places that seem to reach for me in an unexpected way.
Maybe because my religious emotions have seldom
been fed by churches or temples, the places where I've
encountered a sense of power in the ground have
mostly been secluded spots in fields or woods or secu-
lar rooms. I recall a ledge on the side of a peak in the
Blue Ridge Mountains. I haven't been back in forty-two
years; but when I was twenty, I climbed there—among
eagles and clouds—and made some fervent-boy vows
about my future (near-impossible vows that I still work
to keep).

I know a cave in Bethlehem in which, for two thousand years, travelers have stooped to touch the spot
where a girl named Miriam bore a son named Yeshua;
I know a tree behind my house against which I leaned
to begin my first novel; I know the dim room and the
iron bed in which I was born. And only a few days ago,
I rode through the scrub north of Santa Fe and paused
in the village of Chimayo. There in a low adobe
church, for nearly two centuries, a stream of men,
women, and children have come to align their damaged bodies or their hopes for others with a palpable
strength inherent in the place—in its crude striking
paintings and the shallow hole in the dry dirt floor of
a small side-room which constitutes the source of Chi-

mayo's mute offer of help. *Mute,* yet near the hole hangs a clutter of no-longer-needed crutches and canes, the plaster cast from a baby's shattered ankle, a great deal else (though not my wheelchair), and many written claims of thanks.

I first came here three years ago, after I'd surfaced from my own fight. Any part of my luck not owing to humans hadn't come from a hole in New Mexico; I was there to visit friends. But once in Chimayo, I soon recognized that I'd reached another of those scarce sites in which the Earth seems literally charged—with a force that's at least partly benign, though maybe not entirely: a force that's awesomely unpredictable. On a fourth visit a few days ago, I lit five candles and recalled the names of living friends contending with lymphoma, breast cancer, AIDS, and the desolation of a crumbling marriage.

Do I feel their odds are improved by my act? Do I think *my* chances, a few days from now when I undergo my yearly scan for cancer, are stronger after this silent pause? In the words of a strong black man who helped rear me, I've learned not to "put my mouth" on such hopes. All the same, like most of my frail species, I more than half suspect that the Earth— in a very few unlikely places—has pierced itself and streamed real power.

1995

TEACHERS

Wherever I am, the slanting light toward any year's end calls up a long run of near unblemished memory—the recollection of my nineteen years in schools and universities. I not only had the luck to receive those years of training (most of it free), my mind also dealt me the huge good fortune of being a boy who loved the whole idea of school and was immensely susceptible to teachers.

Growing up in Depression years, in a poor stretch of the South, I entered school at the age of six years and seven months. There were no nurseries or kinder-gartens for hundreds of miles round and no television (the one boy in our town who'd learned, on his own, to read at five was acknowledged as a miracle; I used to watch him as if he possessed the power of flight, which of course he did). But when I entered school in September 1939, just as Hitler invaded Poland, I encountered my first caretaker who wasn't either kin or a worker in our home.

I'd experienced qualms that summer, guessing that

the happiness of childhood was ending—unblocked access to my parents' attention, my freedom to roam the woods, then come in and draw my careful pictures of elephants, gorillas, and mountains: pictures that were as true as I could make them, not the daubs of "self-expression" some children paraded before their luckless parents.

But on my first day at Park Street School, I was sent to the classroom of Lucy Lee Lovett; and at the sight of her tall body, the pale face and fine hair, my qualms were swamped by her courtly kindness, the gravity with which she received us, and the potent gifts she had to give—chief of which was *reading*. I'd longed to read, as dogs long to talk.

From that day on, till I quit school at twenty-five, I encountered only one bad teacher. Some were better prepared than others, some more inexplicably endowed with the sorcery that makes great teaching an unteachable art and elevates every master teacher into the guild of genuine magi—those rare magnetos who transmit vital skill, the taste for civilized joy, and the very essence of hope itself: the highest gift from one generation to the next.

In retrospect I can see how a majority of my best teachers were compelled to pay for their talent with a vow that's as rare today as classroom mastery itself—the women and men who taught me most about the world were *single* souls, unmarried, uncompanioned: "old maids," "confirmed bachelors" they were called in those days.

And whatever the reason for their single state, the best of them brought their undiluted time and energy straight to the classroom. The sound of just a few of their names goes far to guarantee their forthright strength—Jane Alston, Crichton Davis, Lessie Cogdell, Harold Parker, Florence Brinkley.

But I'll rest my case on a recent letter from one of those heroes, a woman who taught me after her husband had killed himself. By the time I knew her, she'd raised two children who'd grown up and gone; and she'd begun teaching, alone as any rogue lioness. Nearly fifty years later, at the end of her letter, she starts to remind me of a knowledge we share (I've taught too, for nearly four decades). The knowledge she writes of is also a burden—the risky chance of learning to see through the eyes of a child. She puts it this way—"A kinship of love that cannot be expressed . . . a looking from the same window and seeing the glory and electrical fiber of everything God or man made. The same feeling when one is very young of wanting a parent to see what the seeing child is seeing—the magic of life—well doesn't it wear you down though?"

It hasn't worn my great teacher down; she's alive to prove it, as she nears her hundredth year.

1995

WHEELCHAIR TRAVEL

I became paraplegic ten years ago and, since, have spent my waking time entirely in a wheelchair. For five of those years, the country had no uniform code of accessibility for public transportation, for access to public buildings, or for hotel and restaurant accommodations. Then Congress passed a law which was widely trumpeted as emancipation for the millions of Americans who move through our midst with substantial deficits.

While the Act relies almost entirely on the good will of business, I — and many of my disabled colleagues — anticipated rapid improvement in those problems which have easy solution: the arrangement of public toilets, the small alterations in hotel and restaurant logistics which are vastly liberating. Long years later, I'm sad — no, I'm appalled — to say that improvement has lagged inexcusably nationwide.

I can't speak for opportunities which the Act may have created in the job world; but as a citizen whose work requires frequent travel, I can say that—on the road—I still expect to encounter, daily, ridiculous barricades: all of which are the result of either blindness on the part of the able-bodied, greed which prevents their compliance with the Act, or the ignorance and malice of those Americans who'd like to repel any customer whom they think might prove visually offensive to their able-bodied trade (I've apparently been luckier than most; I've encountered only one hotel manager who told me that he didn't seek guests of "my kind").

For now I'll skip the difficulties of vehicular travel or of navigating our hopeless city streets and focus on a regular and predictable frustration—housing on the road. After explaining my simple needs to hotel reservation clerks and being assured of their ability to supply them, I arrive at a check-in desk, often late at night, to find one of two complications. They're generally articulated, by a nervous clerk, in more or less these words:

"Yes, Mr. Price, the computer shows that your reservation called for a handicap-equipped room plus a connecting room for your assistant; but our *afternoon* clerk seems to have rented our only such combination to someone else."

Or "Sorry, Mr. Price, but our computer implies that those two rooms have an inner connecting door, when in fact they do not." In either case the clerk glances away in the desperate wish to dissolve.

In self-defense I've developed a response. Clean

and well-groomed, I sit squarely in my wheelchair, raise my voice slightly above the comfort level, and ask a justified question—"What do you propose to do about this problem you've created for yourself?"

The regulation answer is that the clerk has no authority to propose a solution and—far worse—that no adequate solution exists within the entire large building: standard-size wheelchairs, for instance, cannot pass through the normal hotel bathroom door; not to mention that, when a paraplegic is placed in bed and left alone behind a locked door, the telephone is his only lifeline; and phones fail immediately in most emergencies. Quadriplegics are worse off.

Occasionally, a first-class hotel will apologize and offer their most spacious suite. Only the other day, a twenty-five-story hotel in Nashville was reduced to providing me with a seven-room suite, all because they had only *one* handicapped room with a connecting door; and its occupant was refusing to depart as scheduled. So my assistant and I languished for two nights in Music City's very odd notions of grandeur. Since so much space must be in slim demand, the hotel was probably none the worse off for that lavish concession to the simple needs of one citizen from the millions who share his physical impediment. With a relatively small expenditure, however, that hotel and its hundreds of clones around the nation could quickly convert enough rooms to meet most all needs.

If and when the travel, restaurant, and hotel business decides to do so—and a welcome few have made the changes—I and my colleagues hope that they'll ask for advice from people with personal experience of disability: a grab bar, for instance, placed two inches above or below its best position is worse than useless. My hope is not only shared, it's the presently gutless law of the land, it's the course of plain human compassion, it's long-range fiscal good sense; and the owners of all unadapted real estate may wish to know what we gimps call the upright and walking: you're only the *temporarily abled* yourselves. *Never forget it.*

1995

A SHALLOW PAST

We're so besieged with fake reminders of our past as a nation that we tend to forget how short that past is—and what an unacknowledged blessing that brevity may be. A trip to incredibly spic-and-span Colonial Williamsburg or the tidy site of the first permanent and wretched English-speaking colony at Jamestown or to General Ulysses Grant's terrifyingly stuffed Victorian home in Galena, Illinois is calculated to convince the unwary that the United States—its *white* component anyhow—has an ancient pedigree, comparable to that of Italy or China.

But all those ladies in eighteenth-century silks and modern frameless bifocals, all those strapping lads in knee pants and hose, are misleading you badly and— worse—dangerously. The United States of America, and its various colonial predecessors on this land mass, is between four and eight generations old, depending on your family's longevity. And that may be hopeful news.

I'm in my early sixties, for instance. Thirty-odd
years ago, I was present at a dinner in Georgetown, Virginia where the guests played a game of who could
reach farthest back in time—who had known whom
who had known whom, on backward to Adam and his
sons? I could say that my father's mother, whom I
remember, had met Robert E. Lee. Another of the
guests was a direct descendant of William Cecil, the
founder of that canny line of Britons who have served
the throne since the reign of Queen Bess.

What struck me indelibly, though, was the last guest
to speak. She was Alice Roosevelt Longworth, the
famous—even notorious—daughter of Teddy Roosevelt, a cousin to Franklin and Eleanor; and despite
her bright-eyed charm and wicked tongue, Mrs. Longworth was well advanced in her eighties. As the game
got to her, she said "When Father was in the White
House, we'd often ride out to Mount Vernon of a Sunday. That was before those *ladies* completely took it
over, and it was a lovely place to visit—the broad lawn
down to the river and the tall airy house. The old gen-
tleman who showed you round the place, his father
had rowed Washington across the Delaware."

I was a man well on in my thirties when I heard that,
but to sit two feet from a smiling vital woman whose
mind could leap from a Georgetown dinner in the late
1960s to the frozen Delaware and the Father of Our
Country in 1776 was a salutary shock. By the time I'd
fallen to sleep that night, Mrs. Longworth's surprise
had spurred me to stretch my own shorter reach.

Why stop with the fact that my Grandmother Price
had met General Lee? Wasn't Lee's wife the daughter
of Parke Custis, and wasn't Custis the grandson of
Martha Washington by her first marriage, and hadn't
Parke Custis been reared by Martha and General
Washington at Mount Vernon? Stranger still, hadn't I
spent long hours of my Carolina childhood and early
manhood in the happy presence of a man named
Grant Terry and a woman named Mary Green, each
of whom was almost surely born into slavery? Neither
of them knew their precise age; but if they were born
after actual freedom in 1865, it could only have been
by a very few years—their parents were certainly slaves.
Those slaves had known, at no distant remove, the
brand of men who could buy human beings, ship
them at peril many thousand miles west, and sell them
at auction. And those shrewd traders had known the
fathers who made them slavers; and those fathers had
known their ancestor Cain, Adam's son, the first
brother-killer and father to us all.

Cain, however, never shared with us the rights of
this republic; and when I despair of our chance to survive the hate and blindness that rend us all ways, I try
to take at least brief comfort in recalling how young
this nation still is—a howling stripling, half pardonable
maybe, the family's hope.

1995

EYE LEVEL
TO A WHEELCHAIR

Home from a recent week in New York, I'm reminded of the stranger benefits accruing to regular wheelchair life. The nightmares of urban wheelchair navigation are predictable—streets so broken as to constitute Maginot lines of shuddering bumps, the absence of curb-cuts, the filth that transfers instantly from pavement to wheeling hands and clothes, the fiercely intent drivers whose eyes see nothing beneath the level of their hood ornaments.

What a visiting gimp acquires more slowly is full awareness of the rare gratifying encounters that are mostly invisible to the able-bodied adult. One of the most surprising is a rush of children toward you. Not often on streets but in airports, stores, and hotel lobbies, a child under the age of six will spot you from yards away and run right up to the edge of your chair.

There, they sometimes stall and go blank; but generally they say "Why are you sitting in that?"

I tend to grin and say "My legs don't work." They ask "Why?" and I say "Just lucky I guess." Their response is a solemn "Oh" or a nod. Every so often a child asks to stand on my footrest, and I try to oblige. But why their attraction to a seated white-haired older man? Initially, I've come to think, they're drawn by the sight of an adult who's roughly their height and can meet them eye-to-eye (any veteran of a chair knows how daunting it is to talk *up* at standing adults).

During my recent week in New York, however, the memorable eye-to-eye meetings occurred in the colder hours of dusk and night. It's notorious that Manhattanites navigate their crowded streets under one strict rule—*Never meet another human being's eyes.* The nearest person may be psychotic, a beggar, a serial mugger, a tout for the nearest condom boutique, or a lurking sexual predator. So—as with many of the other higher mammals—the course of prudence is to avoid eye contact. An eye-meet implies a willingness to interact with another person, if only violently. Since resorting to the wheelchair, I've gradually learned to breach that taboo, and with some reward.

On crowded streets, though waist-high to most passers, I note that they often can't resist looking toward my face—presumably to check on the nature of another human's damage. When such a check occurs, I rush to meet the gaze, to hold it a moment, and then

to *grin*—indicating life at least, the absence of immediate suffering, or the arrival of cheerful lunacy. All but
invariably, the furtive gazer shies quickly—and even on
the flintiest New York face—a return smile rises, which
I tend to view as a small benign result.

What's a good deal stranger is another kind of meeting that registered on me in my latest visit as the days
and nights grew shorter and colder. The homeless
men and women of the streets were fast assuming
those extra skins of worn sweaters and battered coats
they'll need for five icy months; even the skin of their
faces and hands is visibly darkening and thickening to
seize any calorie of heat that comes their way. Maybe
to avoid harassment for importuning passers, the
homeless in New York tend to sit on or by curbstones
or propped against buildings; so I meet them—like the
children—at eye level.

And my discovery was this—never once in my
eleven seated years, in city or town, has a single homeless man or woman asked anything of me. Oh, occasionally there's the silent request of a hand-printed
sign. Fifth Avenue, for instance (with its lavish shops),
has one or two men who sit by signs that say VIETNAM
VET WITH AIDS—but I can't recall a single hand that's
reached toward me, or any begging word, though
friends beside me are frequently asked. When the eyes
meet mine, and they often do, I sense a flicker of
greeting.

Am I fabricating or is it fraternity; in those piercing
eyes am I somehow exempt as more of a brother than

the upright and swift? Beside their uninsistent existence, their bottomless misery, I know again I'm a
pampered child. And they pass me a question they
never ask—*What justice lies in wait for a nation that
walks or rolls in self-sufficiency past this many freezing
and roofless creatures: our actual kin?*

1995

PRIVATE WORSHIP

Country and small-town churches were important to my family always — as they were to me, on into manhood. But when I finished my undergraduate years at Duke, with its vaulting chapel, and left for three years of further study in England, I found myself withdrawing from public worship, except for weddings and funerals. There was certainly no lack of magnificent cathedrals and churches in Britain; no, what was working in me — I think — was a half-conscious reaction to a delayed admission that the Christian churches of my native region were mired to the eyes in the ancient and alarmingly vital brand of racism that (in those days) seemed peculiar to the states of the old Confederacy.

Nothing in America then was whiter than the churches of my youth. Even today, forty years after my withdrawal, it remains largely correct to say that no hour in the South — and in most of the country (as I now know) — is more segregated than eleven o'clock on Sunday morning. Yet it's worth recalling what I only realized after my withdrawal—like many Americans, I deduced my qualms about racism, to a large extent, from what the church had taught me of the ethics of the Hebrew prophets and Jesus.

What I never lost in these years of withdrawal is a rock-ribbed sense that I—like all the world—am the willed creation of a single power whom I, and most Americans, think of as God. I've also persisted in an early ingrained belief that the man Jesus bore a unique relation to the creator, a relation which continues to offer me and millions of others both light and meaning. But when I've occasionally felt a need to give myself another chance at organized worship, I've been repelled again—by my old qualms and a few strong new ones.

I can't help noticing that the mainline white churches of America are still—speaking generally now—among the strongest bastions of intolerance and lethal self-righteousness. An hour of fiddling with the radio or TV on a Sunday morning can be a chilling experience in hearing the voices of hate and fear pour out of buildings that claim to be founded in mercy and trust—buildings situated everywhere from the poor side of town to the gilded suburbs.

The flaw in my logic is obvious. Anyone who's repelled by normal human failings, however awful, might best combat them by working for change from the inside out, from the core of the problem in those numerous minds who nonetheless bring themselves regularly into what they think of as the presence of God. I confess the grave flaw; but still when I've tried to swallow my scruples and find a church, I'm invariably confronted by this fairly new American phenomenon—the church as country club.

I attend in the hope of quiet engagement with the mystery of the world and my fellows, and I'm met with invitations to join what amounts to a social club— the men's encounter group, the potluck supper, the boys' and girls' soccer teams, the choir, the seniors' trip to Israel or Rock City. I'm certain that a careful search would find me a place where communal worship was possible without a social calendar, but by now I'm set in a four-decade habit.

I'm even convinced that my lone Sunday mornings are more than a habit; they fill a profound need in my by no means exotic nature—again, a need for private engagement with ultimate mystery. The rest of my week, I plow my worship into writing my books, teaching my students, and living with friends and enemies in whatever decency I can muster (which is not enough). Am I bound for Hell in a swift handbasket? Many think so. But sure as I am of a lifetime's errors, I never feel more deeply at home on this blue planet—in the whole universe—than in those solitary moments, trying to face the mind of God in a grove of trees.

1996

GONE WITH THE WIND
AND ITS SCARLETT

In the spring of 1940, I was in first grade in a small mill town in central Carolina when my parents fetched me out of school; and we went to the local reserved-seat premiere of *Gone With the Wind*. I have awed memories of my first exposure to a work of popular art so strong in its narrative flood; and whenever I've watched it since—as I recently did in TNT's replay—I'm held in willing bondage till the whole length has rolled on through me. So when I encounter those frequent polls in which film critics solemnly list admittedly worthy movies like *Citizen Kane* or *Potemkin* as the best of all time, I'm prone to smile and cast my vote with the majority of human watchers— the greatest film success, in every way, is *Gone With the Wind*.

The sources of its power, over nearly six decades of international audiences—a power exerted by no other

film over so long a span—have been ceaselessly ana-
lyzed: the brisk hypnotic pace of its storytelling, the
grounding of its full-blown emotion in an actual and
immensely tragic war, the brilliance of its technical
skills (sets, costumes, music, photography, a painterly
use of Technicolor superior to any visible today), and
its perfect cast.

In my latest watch, I tried hard to fault the performances of Gable, De Havilland, Leslie Howard, Hat-
tie McDaniel, Butterfly McQueen, and the others.
But—grant them their tradition of romantic acting
and their native time (which was America toward the
end of the Depression, on the brink of the Second
World War); and their achievements remain
unmatched for intelligence, range, depth, wit, and a
ravenous vitality unlike that available to any other
collection of players known to me.

But despite the praise which she won as Scarlett
O'Hara, Vivien Leigh has never been fully acknowledged for what she—at the age of twenty-five—managed to find within herself: the richest response to the
largest challenge ever thrown a film actress. Through
nearly four hours and a narrative stretch of more than
a decade, Leigh is the center of virtually every scene;
and whether we see her in the chattering flirtations of
late adolescence, in the folly of her fixation on a man
who cannot love her, in her burning defiance of war
and subsequent torment, or in the slow destruction of
her illusions, she enlivens every frame with a protean
physical beauty and—more important—with an

uncanny watchfulness and a lightning speed of mental and emotional response.

No wonder she's often remembered as a species of cat—a sleek Siamese or, more precisely, a gorgeous and genuinely dangerous leopard. So complete and detailed is Leigh's identification with Scarlett's life that it's worth watching the film through at least once, fixed entirely on her face. I tried that just now; and the focus and heat of her intensity never flag an instant, even in moments when excellent actors elsewhere in the scene go blank as humans often do.

To dwell on intensity as her prime result, however, is to slight her gift for sly comedy and to simplify the use she makes of her totally functional beauty, a beauty that nearly became her curse. Through the remainder of her career, in film and on stage, the seriousness of Vivien Leigh's dedication and the success of her results were often discounted as the second-class accompaniments of an accidentally glamorous woman. Even if such performances as her Lady Hamilton, Cleopatra, and Blanche Dubois did not belie such meanness, it's worth insisting that an anatomical gift of beauty, however phenomenal, would have abandoned her by early adulthood if she had not gone on earning her gift through intelligent discipline and the inner grace which cannot be bought or hired—recall the truism that "After early youth, we all have the face we deserve."

Vivien Leigh's husband, Laurence Olivier, was the premier actor of the English-speaking stage and film for much of his long life. Her own life—har-

rowed by tuberculosis and manic-depression—burnt
itself out before she was fifty-four, but her accom-
plishment in *Gone With the Wind* (should she have
left nothing else behind her) serves amply to explain
not only the success of the film but likewise to show
her as Olivier's equal and the flaming unforgettable
phoenix among her other peers. If you're feeling the
draining tooth of winter, go rent her great triumph
and feed on her life.

1996

NATIVE ORPHANS

There's been a great swell of praise lately for three new filmed adaptations from the novels of Jane Austen — novels written in early nineteenth century England by an Englishwoman and filmed for the large screen and television by her modern countrymen. All of which is fine by me, but it's been a long while since I heard a single word of lament that the almost infinitely wealthier media of American film and television continue their baffling neglect, their apparent scorn, of the waiting riches of American literature: particularly some century-and-a-half of splendid homegrown novels and plays.

Look down the American fiction and drama shelves of your nearest library; locate the absolute first-class titles from James Fenimore Cooper, Hawthorne, Melville, Mark Twain on through Willa Cather, Eugene O'Neill, Hemingway, Faulkner, and Fitzgerald to Tennessee Williams, Ralph Ellison, Saul Bellow, Toni Morrison, and their live-and-kicking peers. Search your

memory for a single example of a first-class film adapted
from any classic American novel or play—a *first-class*
film now, not a merely dutiful or mildly admirable
gesture.

My own recent search turns up only three such
unassailable achievements—Sidney Lumet's version
of O'Neill's *Long Day's Journey into Night*, John Ford's
version of Steinbeck's *The Grapes of Wrath*, and
Michael Mann's recent version of Cooper's *Last of the
Mohicans*. Period. Oh, I may have forgot a contender
or two; I'll even concede you Martin Scorsese's over-
stuffed waxwork of Edith Wharton's *Age of Innocence*.
And all right, I'll admit to passing up Demi Moore in
the new and happy-ending *Scarlet Letter*; I'm well
aware of the many TV and movie classic duds (all the
Hemingway films for instance) and of dozens of fine
films made from lesser novels—films like *Gone With
the Wind* and *The Big Sleep*—but I don't expect to
hear a chorus of reminders of the brilliance I've
neglected to mention.

You, like me, must switch on your television occasionally—or scan the movie ads—in hopes of some
diversion that might satisfy at least a normal twelve-
year-old, only to find as I do (and I possess a satellite
dish with hundreds of channels) the same unending
root-canal ache of idiotic porno-violence or situation
comedy of nursery-school depth. Switch to the small
array of "cultural" channels (including our own woe-
fully underfunded and sadly unadventurous public
television system) or again consult movie ads, and

what will you find? — dutiful and occasionally gratifying English-made adaptations of English drama and
fiction, from *Brideshead Revisited* in the early 1980s to
the recent *Middlemarch*. At the movies, you can soon
watch new versions of such ancient TV gems as
McHale's Navy and *Flipper*. Whereas, only last year
PBS canceled *American Playhouse*, its sole venture
devoted to new and classic American televised drama.

What's the cause? We've plainly developed a
motion picture and television industry unparalled in
the world for its technical competence; the country is
groaning with young and old scriptwriters of proven
excellence or obvious promise who are begging to
work, on adaptations or their own creations. Any contact with the American school population, from first
grade through college, reveals a dire and punishing
ignorance of our literary heritage — a heritage whose
richness, vitality, and wisdom might well induce pride
and ambition in any number of our dangerously dis-
affected young.

And for all the recent assaults on our minuscule
federally funded arts programs, the country is awash
with private and corporate wealth that might be
intelligently solicited and then marshaled by gifted
producers and artists into further native resources of
incalculable value to the present and the future of
the republic.

Think of only a few possibilities — a film of Willa
Cather's masterpiece *A Lost Lady*, a serious multipart
version of William Faulkner's related Yoknapatawpha

novels, Eudora Welty's most elegant novel *Delta Wedding*, the deeply scored chronicle of African-American resourcefulness in Toni Morrison's *Song of Solomon*, William Kennedy's Albany cycle, Robert Stone's parable of American havoc overseas in A *Flag for Sunrise*, Shelby Foote's epic narrative trilogy of the Civil War and onward through a multitude of stories for the next millennium—why not?

What's to lose in that hope and its rapid fulfillment? Only a national laziness of staggering depth; only the layers of lard with which commercial film and TV have smothered our minds; only the ongoing fury of hundreds of thousands of young Americans swamped like us all in a media diet of so-far bottomless greed and cynicism. Where, today, is a first volunteer to start the funding and the first round of redeeming pride?

1996

MY TOLERANCE PROBLEM

An overwhelming majority of Americans claim
to adhere to one or more of the world religions — Hin-
duism, Buddhism, Judaism, Christianity, Islam. To
the best of my understanding, each of those systems of
belief enjoins love of one's neighbor and mercy to
that neighbor as the prime value in human relations.
For example, the God of Hebrew and Christian scripture plainly says that vengeance is his prerogative, not
ours. He tells us, quite flatly, not to kill.

But if your experience resembles mine in the past
few years, you encounter in daily American life an
increasing and ferociously expressed craving for
revenge on whomever the individual speaker defines
as his or her enemy. Virtually every time a widely
sought killer is arrested, television treats us to the sight
of the family of that killer's victim; and more often than
not, those understandably anguished people demand
that the killer suffer death at the hands of the state.
They often add, most disturbingly, "though that's not

good enough for what he or she did." And seven states of the union now permit family members of a murdered victim to witness the killer's execution. Which state will be first to offer the bereaved bystanders the right to throw the actual death switch?

I recall last year—at the arrest of Susan Smith for the drowning of her two sons in Union, South Carolina—that a pleasant-looking young man was shown outside Smith's jail, expressing a simple and by no means un-American wish: "Just turn her over to me for an hour."

Not that I think such responses are uniquely American. A cry for vengeance is widespread throughout the Earth. But given our claim to be a God-fearing nation—in light of the violence rife among us, and given local television's bottomless appetite for defining the news as bloody sensation—an observant American can hardly fail to sense an alarming rise in the rate of blood-lust among us.

Think only, for another recent example, of the father of Ron Goldman at the O.J. Simpson trial. Aside from any question of Simpson's guilt or innocence, and however sympathetic to the Goldman family's ghastly loss of a son, I found myself puzzled by Mr. Goldman's enraged cries for justice—his vision of justice. But how is a tragically lost son to benefit from such a cry? And if bone-deep ultimate punishment is the aim, as it appears to be, of so many similar cries for justice, then what heavier punishment can be imagined than to spare a Susan Smith the death chair and award her the rest of her natural life, apart from the world in guarded confinement, with ample time to contemplate the lives that her young sons will not have? That is, in fact, her sentence; and what human sentence could exceed such a curse?

Have I grown excessively tolerant with age and with my own bill of mainstream but sizable guilts? What would be lost if there were fewer prisons and literally no death-penalty machines in America? Undeniably there are incurable psychopathic murderers, child molesters, and professional criminals whom the public has a right to want removed from our midst. There are likewise numerous sane citizens who are deterred from acts of violence and from white-collar crime by the mere existence of the threat of public punishment.

But does the existence of evil and crime demand that so many law-abiding citizens abandon their professed ethics and bellow their enraged cries for blood? Isn't such an obsession with the tragic events of one's own past history only another stage on the way toward a savage distrust of all strangers and a raucous demand that every felony and sin be met with a civil violence which is far more threatening to our national health than most personal wrongs? What if a whole large nation, for once, were to act as God requires when he says quite calmly—again in Hebrew and Christian scripture—"I will have mercy and not sacrifice" and "Revenge is mine; I will repay"?

1996

A SINGLE DEATH
AMONG MANY

The Centers for Disease Control have recently
confirmed that, for three years now, AIDS has been
the leading cause of death for all American citizens
between the ages of twenty-five and forty-four. The
killer likewise devastates the younger and older
among us, in most ethnic groups and all sexual identities. This news of another triumph for AIDS may
sound numbing to those who've so far escaped its
grasp. But hundreds of thousands know how appalling
it is to watch helpless as a friend, a mate, a child, a
kinsman is clawed to the ground, then eaten—cell by
cell—by a single breed of unimaginably resourceful
virus.

Till recently I'd lost four close friends to its hunger—
a theatrical director, a teacher, a photographer, and a
culinary writer. For reasons pertaining to geographical
distance and to my own battle with cancer, I was

unable to offer those friends real help. In the past eighteen months, however, I've been in regular touch with a friend succumbing to AIDS. As his strength waned slowly, we'd meet for hours and—amid much laughter and without quite admitting what we were doing—I'd gently urge my friend to tell me whatever he wanted to be known of his fading life. He was forty-eight years old and would readily reply with memorable stories of a blazing high vitality. We last met five days before his death; and shortly thereafter, I attended his funeral.

He sported the perfect name—Lightning Brown. For twenty years, Lightning worked in Chapel Hill, first as a scholar of German literature, finally as a lawyer. And in all his aspects, his slim form was a mastiff battler for individual rights and tolerance and for the rights of the Earth herself to be as unspoiled as humans can ensure. An amazing number of times, Lightning's hope for small decencies won the day in a region as likely as any to fail.

His bear-trap mind was fitted with an honest politician's battery of gears. He could be furiously unrelenting in his pursuit of what he saw as the ends of justice. A veteran of the student generation of the 1960s at the University of Oregon, he was a deafening howler when howling seemed productive. Yet he could shift at an instant's notice to the gentler modes of minutely attentive friendship and relaxed exchanges of wit and encouragement, not to speak of his broad knowledge of German and American poetry.

With all his interests and passions, in the final year of his life—harrowed as he was—he focused keenly and wrote many striking poems. None is more haunting than these few lines he wrote for the AIDS House in Carrboro where he spent his last weeks—

> Come on over, maybe death will be here
> he works four days a week
> sometimes visiting in the rooms
> sometimes just walking around the corridors
> I suppose for exercise
> I suppose he likes it here
>
> Have a seat and take off your tight shoes
> So comfortable, so assuring
> you could go barefoot forever

Lightning died in that house, ringed by his parents, sisters, brothers, and the friends who could bear to face his ruined body. Dozens more attended his memorial, and I had the sad privilege to join his family on a snow-driven morning as they scattered his ashes. Home that noon, I wrote a poem of my own—to fix the moment and to mitigate the sights of the hard ending of a creature as worthy as any from the masses consumed already or marked for a similar lingering death by a fate as awful as the human race has known. The poem is called "Scattering Lightning in the Slave Cemetery in Chapel Hill"—

What white man on the planet but you
Would think to be strewn on the wide-spaced graves
Of human chattel, men and women
Enslaved by the local faculty, clergy,
Some century and a half ago?
Yet seeing the place in this driving snowstorm —
Old pines thicker than elephant thighs,
A squat wall, jagged fieldstone markers
(Bare of names) to a few dozen lives
Voiceless to speak the still inexplicable
Fact of bondage in a whole town chartered
For freedom and mercy—you seem a fit occupant,
Parched to essence by a fire you kindled
Knowingly in the midst of a life
Already smoking, hell-bent on justice
For the birthright-helpless and the Earth herself.
   We strew your sandy ochre dust,
The two slim quarts we'll all come to,
On frozen wind that blows you back
Against our legs before you settle;
And I recall your last four words
As you fined your aim down toward the end —
"Am I there yet?"
               There, lost pal.
There at the least.

                           1996

THE MAD INVENTOR

One of the dumber daily radio serials of my childhood was called "Lorenzo Jones and His Wife, Belle." Lorenzo was a harmless crackpot, constantly perfecting the next-to-last version of some invention that the world was decidedly not waiting for. A number of products which Americans can actually buy today are Lorenzo-esque in their looney pointlessness — the battery-powered pepper mill, the rotary nose-hair trimmer, the heated jumpsuit for dogs and cats.

And with age I find myself waking in the night every few weeks — always after an enormous dinner — with what feels like a brilliant and much needed contraption, one that I (with only a little help from appropriate colleagues) could perfect and market for stupendous returns. So urgently does their development loom before me that I'm prepared to risk, here and now, the secrets of my craft if only to share with you the excitement of their imminence. So far there are three hot projects.

The first—home liposuction—is an idea whose time is far past overdue. In its attractive portable case, the unit can sit at your bedside, in your bath or kitchen, ready at a touch (and after, admittedly, a tiny painless incision in your midriff), to hose off the excess fat of a summer barbecue, a week at your mother's, or an all-night luau. No embarrassing visit to the cosmetic-surgery ward, no wait at all.

Second—the skin, or flesh, zipper—will surely prove a satisfying last-ditch resort when even home liposuction can no longer keep pace with that midlife metabolic revolution which lowers your metabolism rate and makes weight control largely a matter of tears or desperate laughter. Under light anesthesia, a heavy-duty long-life plastic zipper is installed along your waistline, thighs, or saddlebags. Then on future occasions when you're tempted by a slab of prime steak or a wodge of chocolate cream pie, avoid the tiresome necessity of biting, chewing, and swallowing by simply opening the skin zipper and inserting the steak or pie into the growing midriff or buttocks.

My third project is still in the early stages of development, but it may prove to be the ultimate bonanza. Presently called the calorie-exchange switch, it will likewise be implantable by minor same-day surgery. Once in place, it will permit you—by only a small flip of the external switch—to reverse your metabolism from its *input* to its *output* mode. Bored by that soused old fullback at the high-school reunion? Trapped by that chatterbox matron at the book club? As each leans

toward you with ferocious spiritual hunger, why surrender to him or her those precious grams of your
psychic vitality, the very meat of your soul?

Instead, with an unobtrusive flick of your finger, trip
that switch behind your ear and—instead of glazed
eyes or verbal scorn—give your starved friend (in a
painless interchange of energy) a calibrated rush of
actual calories. Award the wattled fullback fifty thousand calories; give the withered matron a generous
hundred thousand. Think again of that romantic cook-
out on the beach—soon you can return from your
well-fed week on the water a newer trimmer you: a you
minus fifteen or twenty pounds. Only your calorie-
exchange switch will know!

Further bulletins as the projects mature.

1996

SUMMER VACATION

A friend of mine claims that middle-class veterans of American public education take years after final graduation to comprehend that they no longer get school vacations. Since I've taught for the past four decades, I've had the luxury of those frequent pauses, above all the three months of summer freedom. At the start of my career, an older teacher said to me, not entirely in jest, "There are three main reasons for being a teacher—June, July, and August."

And in the early years, when I taught full-time, those three reasons were crucial to the health of my other profession—writing fiction, poems, essays, and plays. I recall vividly the dripping swelter as I sat chained to my desk through those summers in the unairconditioned trailer where I lived in central North Carolina. A born Tarbaby, I gloried in the heat; my first novel was being literally sweated out of me.

But the peak of my summer memories comes from further back—the endless hushed summers of the late

1930s and forties, especially those years when we lived
in the country or when I spent slowed-down indolent
weeks with relatives in a country village. It was one of
the numerous forms of grace that I experienced from
a by-no-means highly educated mother and father—
I had no siblings until I was eight; and when playtime
came, they wisely left me alone. Apparently they
assumed that, with a normal child's brain and a few
inexpensive books and toys, I could make my own
world and my own life in it. A loving child, I rewarded
them by doing so.

It was both a solitary and an elaborately compan-
ioned venture. Instead of human playmates my age, I
had a loyal and communicative dog; the large array of
wild birds, reptiles, and mammals that were available
in a nearby small suburban forest; and I had my bur-
geoning imagination. On a narrow base of stories I'd
read in *The Boy's King Arthur,* in *Treasure Island* and
a Bible-story book, in the Tarzan and Indian movies I'd
seen, every clear day I staged with keen appetite stories
of danger and ultimate rescue in which—almost
always—I played all roles.

And no memory surpasses the moment when at
the age of six, in the midst of being an Indian alone
with my hunting knife, I plunged that knife into the
bark of a pine tree, suddenly bit the iron blade, and
waited—as I'd seen Tonto do—for the sound of buffalo
in the earth. What came instead was a flooding word-
less realization that I was not now, nor never would be,
truly alone—that this whole visible and invisible world

around me was a single vast teeming organism of which I was a young and slender but important part. I didn't know for years that such genuinely valid mystic experiences are not uncommon among children who've been given half a chance at meaningful silence.

Not that I avoided the company of my contemporaries. During the school year, on our huge playground, I ran with them in almost excessive delight. And sometimes in the summers, one of my classmates or my cousins Marcia and Pat would come out and join me for more thickly populated outdoor theatricals. The memories of those happy times are as strong as my memories of solitude, but I think I know that the solitary hours were far more valuable as preparation for the typical human future I'd get—with prodigious highs and lows.

In the students I teach at a first-rate university today, I notice the triumph of a disturbing herd mentality or at least a tribal compulsion: a puerile form of totemism sustained by appallingly large doses of alcohol and potentially lethal sexual buccaneering (male and female). When I contemplate that near-paralyzing addiction to company and the fear of solitude that drive so many Americans today, I feel hugely grateful for the thousands of solitary summer days in my childhood.

So often, as at the recent arrest of the Unabomber suspect, we're told that such and such a monster adult was a "loner" as a child. "Lonerism" is un-American. I should probably, then, not claim to be the republic's sanest asset; but God knows, I thank my parents and my early fate for those summer vacation years as a single child, alone as a hawk in the broadest sky to make my world in the sun and the richly inhabited greenery, woods that were as wild to me as the heart of the Congo and have proven at least as instructive in the rules of decent existence as any human being I've known in a lucky lifetime's friendships.

1996

A FULL DAY

In the years of the Great Depression, my family hardly suffered the grim dislocation of so many Americans in the desperate search for work and food; but my father's jobs as a salesman of electrical appliances did move us around the state of North Carolina a good deal more often than I—a child who badly wanted roots—could enjoy. One of my early pieces of luck however was that we settled for eight years in one town, Asheboro. There at the age of six, I entered the first grade of public school, met dozens of likable children, and proceeded happily through the first five grades. Then much against my eleven-year-old will, in 1944 we moved away; and I was pried apart from my first real friends—those primal figures from my childhood whom no later acquaintance has quite matched in magnetism and sheer amazement.

I missed my teachers and friends so much—the safe green streets of a small textile-mill town with its huge park and dark cool movie-palaces—that for many

years I couldn't trust myself to revisit the place. I sup-
pose I thought I might burst into sobs and refuse to
return to my parents. If I had, there'd have been several families who'd have taken me in. As it was, I never
again saw those pristine friends. Not until recently. For
the past year, Asheboro has been celebrating the bicen-
tennial of its founding; and the mayor kindly invited
me back to talk about my memories. At the age of sixty-
three, I thought I just might risk encountering some of
those long-lost faces and I went.

  The arrangements had been made with uncanny
perfection. A picnic supper was set in the backyard of
the last apartment house my family lived in before
leaving. A dozen former schoolmates were there; and
my memory for faces—aging though it is—was able to
call their names at once. At the very least, they'd fared
no worse than I. When we moved on to my talk, not
only was the auditorium of the community college
studded with further welcome faces—even the woman
who'd sold me my first pair of school shoes—but the
first "best friend" of my life introduced me.

  He'd come all the way from Pennsylvania for the
reunion (he's a distinguished vascular surgeon there).
We hadn't laid eyes on one another in fifty-two years;
but we were each quickly swamped in floods of
detailed recollection—his handmade set of King
Arthur and the Round Table Knights, my handmade
Tarzan loincloth. At the end of my talk, numbers of
other familiars crowded round; and—again, astonishingly—my otherwise porous memory produced their

names and early histories unfailingly. All their recollections proved as extraordinary in clarity as mine.

In the two-hour drive back home that night, I felt the almost unbearable elation of childhood joy. Why, after a hyphen as long as fifty-two years? There were surely dozens of causes; but after a few weeks' reflection, I now suspect that my long-separated friends and I shared that beautiful affirmation which illumines the end of several of Shakespeare's late plays. The world — with all its thirst for blood, havoc, breach, and permanent severance — will sometimes choose to lure us forward into a small ring of radiance and to share with us there those kinfolk, colleagues, and friends whom we've lost and never thought to see again.

In the days since my flawless Asheboro reunion, I've dreamt for the first time in a very long while those dreams that followed the deaths of my mother and father, thirty and forty years ago — dreams in which I walk through the door of a small party of acquaintances and suddenly glimpse, ten yards away, one or the other of my parents, obviously alive again: young and charming, heads tossed back in laughter. Six decades of life, bountiful as they've been, have offered me nothing better.

1996

LUCKY CATCHES

Eleven years ago, after I'd spent ignorant and hapless months as a paraplegic, a neurologist told me what I was almost ready to hear—I must take a grip on my shattered life, enter a physical rehabilitation unit, and stay till I'd learned to use what strengths the spinal cancer had left me. Dreading the pain and humiliation inevitable in such a choice, I entered the rehab unit of Duke Hospital.

We thirty-odd gimps had our own ward. Each of us had a private room, but we spent our days in the same gym, and we ate together. As expected, the first workouts stretched my scars, my radiation burns, and my unworked muscles; and the effort raised my high pain level to unimagined heights. Unable to reach the toilet, I occasionally suffered mishaps (as did my colleagues); and after a couple of days of tender treatment by the staff, I encountered an unwelcome but desperately needed tone of tough realism.

I doubt I'll forget the moment when I'd fallen to the

floor in the attempt to prove to my therapist that I could still walk. She stood above me and said "Mr. Price, walking is no longer a practical option." In another few days, I'd forced myself to honor her candor and to accept everything I could possibly take from these mysteriously dedicated young men and women. And after a month, I left with a huge store of invaluable knowledge and—better still—with hope for a useful and enjoyable life in a wheelchair.

In my early months of paraplegia, before rehab, I'd turned to anyone for help with even the smallest physical needs—opening doors, retrieving objects from the floor, pouring cups of hot coffee. I was using my paralysis as an excuse for sloth, one of the chief breeders of self-pity. On leaving rehab, however, I sped to the opposite end of the spectrum. Like many men and women suddenly paralyzed, I became virtually belligerent about offers of help. More than a decade later, with some degree of mellowing, I'm less doctrinaire in my demand to serve myself whenever possible.

I've also discovered that it's one of the embarrassing dilemmas for the able-bodied when they encounter one of us who has problems with strength and motion—what should the able-bodied stranger offer to do for us? Plainly there's no established code for offering help to a disabled person. But wisdom would seem to lie, as it does in most relations, in an instant-by-instant sequence of watchful choices.

If you encounter an unaccompanied paralyzed person, a blind person, or anyone else who seems in need,

you might at the least approach the person calmly —
not touching the person's body unless asked to do
so — and suggest that you'd be glad to assist in crossing
a street, helping a wheelchair over a curb, opening a
door, holding an elevator. Don't assume without asking however that the person needs your help. There
are, as I've said, a small minority of us who are committed to self-service and will refuse your offer. Wish
us well in silence.

My experience with the jungle of barriers in all
cities suggests that your calm offer will be accepted.
My wheelchair for instance recently struck a deep
gap in a New York City pavement; and I was pitched
forward onto my knees, rapidly bound to strike the con-
crete, full force on my face. Two quick-witted black
adolescents caught me, deftly and easily. They barely
lingered to hear my thanks. But you might make your
own save, any day. You might help an unheralded
young person who'll live to become a benefactor of the
Earth. And the elderly may reward you equally with
nothing more than that spark of thanks which is still
the most welcome gift of our species.

1996

CASTING BREAD

In no other trades but teaching and the clergy must you be content to cast your bread on the waters of life with no guarantee whatever of return. So I'd be in favor of a rigorous licensing system for would-be teachers if I didn't fear political or religious pressure on the process. Given the intellectual, emotional, and physical outlay that comes with a classroom job, it's a career that shouldn't be attempted by anyone without at least the early glimmers of the complex skills required.

First, because teaching is a performing art. If you can't stand before a restless group and rivet their attention, then you're fated to be the kind of drone whom students rightly flee. If your method reaches only the attentive student, then you must either invent new methods or declare yourself a failure. So must the actor, the priest or nun, the musician whose efforts fall short of reaching the majority of an audience.

My own decades of teaching have been spent in university classrooms. There a teacher seldom encounters the hostility that many public school teachers face. Yet the indifference on the faces of a surprising number of college students can be daunting. A teacher of younger adolescents can hope that his students will outgrow their problems. A college teacher wonders if a truculent student will ever acquire an open mind. Submitting your hopes to so many fish-eyed gazes will require bizarre levels of sadomasochism if you aren't committed to the worth of the gamble.

My impulse to teach came in the third year of high school. Till then, my teachers had been mostly women who faced their tiny paychecks and the galley-slave conditions of their jobs with lavish investments of delight in thankless kids. Crowning their example, I encountered (when I was sixteen) a teacher of unique originality. Her name was Phyllis Peacock; and by an amazing sorcery, she managed to convert her interest in my essays and poems into a yearning in me to write for the rest of my life. And while she never urged a teaching career upon me, my exposure to her refusal to fail left me eager to join her useful tribe of elders. I'd write prose and verse and I'd teach.

So I did and, in the face of ongoing discouragements and pleasures, lately I've begun to trust in real returns (however unreliable) from the honest bread I've cast on the waters. To name only two—I, who've sired no children, have not only worked at the fitting out of several thousand students, I also have an annual

chance to share my time with responsive citizens from
the age of eighteen to twenty-odd when many of my
contemporaries have lost touch with their physical
offspring.

The highest reward of teaching, however, comes in
a form the teacher can only wait for. Few students
ever contact you once they've departed the classroom.
I've had the luck to hear old students quote back to me
some phrase of encouragement I'd long forgot. Again,
those returns are not bankable-on. But a recent letter
from a student, who worked with me in 1960, might
constitute sufficient repayment should I never hear
again.

The student is writing—out of the blue after total
silence—about our study of poetry when she was eighteen and I was twenty-seven. She says "I've found
myself wondering . . . how you taught the poetry of
Gerard Manley Hopkins to 18-year-old girls for whom
despair was not having a date for Friday night. . . . We
must have . . . begun to learn by imitation: being
moved not so much by the poetry as by . . . the intimate
nature of your own engagement with it. . . . It was a gift
I cherish still." And she concludes with what is surely
not merely thanks to me but to other teachers who
stand behind her. "I would like you to know . . . that I
am careful about what I read. I cannot anticipate reading certain things, such as . . . some of Shakespeare's
sonnets, without a sense of risk. I know from experience what can happen to me, or the world, or the day."

What she means is that beauty can happen. A

thoughtful life susceptible to joy can happen in a moment to a well-stocked mind. Write your own letter to your own teacher soon.

1996

MRI TIME

I've recently observed an important anniversary. I've just had my tenth annual MRI scan at Duke Hospital. MRI means *magnetic resonance imaging*. When I was first operated on in 1984, the MRI had not reached major American hospitals. Guided only by X ray, my surgeon was unable to remove the growing malignant tumor that stretched down my spinal cord for ten inches. And the only therapy that a great hospital could offer was five weeks of daily radiation. That huge dose left me paraplegic. But it stalled the tumor for two years, by which time an ultrasonic laser scalpel was available; and the MRI machines were in place. With those aids, in two marathon operations my brilliant surgeon removed all the tumor that he could find.

The second of those laser expeditions occurred late in 1986; and ever since, my surgeon has prescribed an annual MRI scan. He says he doesn't anticipate trouble but wants to stay ahead of any ominous developments at my body's core. So on a recent Monday night, I rolled into the radiology unit and responded to the usual check sheet of warnings Did I have metal plates in my body, iron filings in my eyes, a pacemaker, a penile prosthesis; was I perhaps pregnant?

Certifying my purity, I surrendered to the gentle technicians who are by now old friends; and I spent the next two hours inside that claustrophobe's nightmare—the six-foot-long, twenty-five-inch-wide tube of a magnet which slowly (and with the decidedly low-tech sound of a fifty-dollar motorboat engine) produces uncannily clear images of the soft tissues of a human body. The gain for medicine and the individual patient is immense; minor drawbacks mount as the minutes tick on.

Given that I've put on weight in my wheelchair, there's not room inside the magnet to raise a hand and scratch an itchy nose. Since the longest of my images requires me to lie still for nine minutes—*still* means I can't even swallow—I've acquired a few techniques for tolerating those close quarters without beginning to rave. I ask the technician to switch off the piped-in music and the ventilation fan; then I lie on my back— with the domed ceiling only four inches above my nose. I shut my eyes and recite the contents of my long-term memory—poems I learned in childhood, one-word mantras that have helped me through hard times, the famous Jesus prayer, and more adult poems (some of Shakespeare's sonnets and Milton's "Lycidas").

What is strangest is that, even inside that circular

eye which is charting the health of my spine (the cord which contained an enormous killer), I've never felt *fear*. *Boredom* yes, *relief* in knowing that a friend sits in earshot to haul me out if the technician vanishes, but never *fear*. Yet I'm by no means a dauntless hero in other respects—I can quail at the prospect of a rickety shower chair—so why have I always felt a curious peace in that coffin?

One reason may be that—after my first few MRIs—I learned that one of its inventors was an old friend of mine, George Radda, a young refugee from Soviet Hungary who came to the college in England where I was a student. Most crucially, though, a special calm seems to protect me in the tube, a trust that has always risen like a clean breeze in those stifling quarters—not that I'll never die or never again know agony—but that for now I roll ahead through life on a benignly thick sheet of ice till I've done all the honest work my mind contains.

One week after this year's scan, for instance, I completed my eleventh novel. And this year's scan was again clear of cancer.

1996

TIME-RIDDEN

My friends often remind me of my obsession with time—I'm always asking people's ages, always celebrating anniversaries; I'm mercilessly prompt. Many Americans prefer not to notice the passage of years; but for someone who writes fiction as I do, time is my subject. Name five of your favorite novels—aren't they mainly concerned with what time does to human beings? The subject pours into my work too—from direct observation of the lives of others and from my lifelong dread of detaining people, missing planes, missing rich encounters.

Of course I'm doomed to have as my friends many men and women who're blithely cavalier with my time. If they're twenty minutes late, they feel no need to phone; they'll *be* there (little do they know that I'm on the verge of phoning the highway patrol to see if their flesh doesn't litter an interstate). I've gone so far as to set out to find the delayed friend; and I've spent my adult life, circling the block before most appoint-

ments—marking time till my hostess can unroll her
sausage curlers.

Otherwise I'm a man of few compulsions. I don't
wash my hands every minute; I don't return to the
house five times to be sure the oven's turned off. My
mania for punctuality, in fact, seldom applies to my
own solitary activities. I don't have to have my own solo
lunch at precisely one o'clock or my two ounces of
unblended Scotch on the tick of five. So how did I
come by this mania where other humans are involved?
There may be unconscious causes in my deep past. I
was for instance an embryo who resisted delivery; I presented my ten-pound butt to the doctor and withstood
his forceps for a whole long night.

But the first cause I'm *sure* about was my father's
inability to keep his word in matters of time; and
before I was five, I'd begun to experience real fear of
his tardiness. Since I adored my father through all
the twenty-one years I knew him, I took the earliest
opportunities to accompany him on his work. He was
a traveling salesman of electrical appliances; and on
occasional mornings before I entered school, he'd ask
if I'd like to ride with him on his calls. Warned though
I'd been, I invariably accepted with glee—only to confront, in a matter of moments, the inevitable quandary.
Father would pull the black Pontiac up in front of a
house, reach for his brochures, say "Darling, sit here
just a minute. This lady needs a floor lamp." I'd say "All
right," and his minute would begin its remorseless
stretching.

He'd knock, a woman in a housedress or an old man in suspenders would answer, Father would offer his blazing smile, the door would shut behind him; and within three minutes, I'd know I was abandoned. Since abandonment is a child's greatest dread—isn't it also the dread of most adults?—I'd wait on in the hot or cold car, dully numbering my courses of action. After how many minutes could I go to the door and ask to see him? What if the man with suspenders had killed him? What if Father and the woman had gone out the back door and left for the moon? How would I find the nearest phone to call the police, and what would I say—*I'm a smart little boy whose father doesn't want him?*

Five decades have passed and I never quite shamed myself. But I never recovered. And before I was six, I'd sworn a silent vow—I *will never keep* anyone *waiting.* Even now, if you expect me at noon, be prepared to see me as the first chime strikes. If you're not there, you've got thirty seconds till I'm a rabid wolverine of fear and enmity. Approach with great care—and with offerings of the finest dark chocolate.

1996

FATHER AND HISTORY

 M y father's formal education ended with
high school, but his sense of American and world history was always strong, and my best memories of him
condense around moments when he took pains to see
that I share his sense of the overarching power of the
past and—above all—the ongoing force of those men
and women who truly bend time. My earliest recollection of his concern comes from 1937, and it's one of
the two most vivid memories I have of his care. I was
four years old. We were visiting his boyhood home in
eastern North Carolina when he rose and announced
to his sisters that he was taking me out to see Aunt Winnie Williams.

My three aunts laughed at his plan—"Aunt Winnie
is so old she won't have any idea who you *are*." Stubborn as ever, Father said "We won't know that till Aunt
Winnie's seen me." And off we went. Like many sons,
I was seldom happier than when Father and I were
alone in a moving car. That feeling of glad nearness sur-

vives with me, but what remains from our actual meeting with Winnie Williams is only the hazy sight of an
ancient woman in an upright chair. She has pale tan
skin with furious tints of a natural blood-red in her
cheeks. As Father moves me shyly toward her, she
reaches out a hand like a bone rake and strokes my fore-
head, mumbling inaudibly. I reach up and touch her.

Back in the car, I ask Father what she said. He tells
me she was "giving me her blessing." And when I ask
why her cheeks are so red, he says "She's more than
half Indian, son — an old woman with Indian blood.
She's nearly a hundred years old now, and she used to
be a slave." In that dim meeting then, in the swelter of
a wood-burning tin stove, my father had laid my hand
against the two prime American tragedies — the mas-
sacre of Indians, the bondage of slaves. And within a
year he'd given me books about both disasters, books
which I waited impatiently to read.

A decade later, after he'd addicted me to sitting at his
side for the evening war news, he took my hand again
and touched me to two other quite different women —
both white and old, both powerful on the world's great
stage. The occasion was the funeral in Raleigh of Jose-
phus Daniels, Woodrow Wilson's Secretary of the Navy.
On a rainy winter day, Father took me to the city's old
Oakview cemetery. After we'd watched the coffin sink,
Father took my arm and — without a word — led me
quickly toward a black limousine. The windows were
rain-streaked, and I couldn't imagine who was inside.

Before I could experience the classic adolescent

horror at a parent's social daring, Father bowed at the near backseat window. And the window lowered. At once I recognized the world's most famous woman; and I heard my father say "Mrs. Roosevelt, I was your husband's great admirer. This is my son Reynolds." Eleanor Roosevelt smiled and with kind dignity extended her hand to me. When I released it, she gestured to the older woman beside her—"Reynolds, this is Mrs. Woodrow Wilson." Mrs. Wilson, a famous beauty in her prime, still had the riveting dark eyes and the graceful command with which she'd virtually run the country during her husband's last illness. She nodded, then smiled as brilliantly as if I were the British ambassador; and she said "Good afternoon, young man."

As we left, I remember looking to Father's gravely fulfilled face. He'd tell me about both women tonight—what I'd need to know and learn. Till then, what I had was Mrs. Woodrow Wilson's voice calling me "young *man.*" No one had called me a man till that moment. That alone was history—and was caused by my father.

1996

THE LUCKY CHILD'S
CHRISTMAS

Since at least the advent of Charles Dickens's Tiny Tim, we've been on notice to think—in the holiday bounty—of those children who're sick, hungry, cold, even homeless. In all the major religions of America, as the year expires in the winter solstice, we're rightly reminded to set the helpless high in our thoughts and actions. We're likewise bombarded with images of luckier children, children surrounded (even inundated) with their year-end bounty: toys, sweets, deep cushions of love.

What I never see noticed is the kind of child I was in the 1930s and early forties when I was still my parents' only offspring and the target of their overwhelming generosity. In those long Depression years, my father was far from well paid; he shifted jobs often; and he, my mother, and I moved incessantly. So whatever my failings, I was not a boy spoiled by wealth or the complacency of a rooted household. I longed for that very rootedness—a steady place of my own in the midst of my family's love—but it would be years before we were grounded in a lasting home.

In the face of that prime uncertainty, my parents labored each Christmas to lavish on me every reasonable gift I asked for—and then something extra—some surprise that would raise my happiness to a pitch that even I had not foreseen. And it was that very hunger of my parents which became the first emotional dilemma I remember. From the time I was four years old, the dilemma arose like this. We'd wake on Christmas morning, my parents would follow me to the lighted tree, and I'd feel the unblinking weight of their eyes as they watched me respond to the blazing outlay of expected gifts. Ungrateful though it may sound, the weight of their gaze was a genuine burden.

That fourth Christmas for instance I'd requested an odd array—an Indian suit (with feathered headdress), a Shirley Temple doll (Shirley was only a little older than I), and an imitation double-barreled shotgun. Santa and my parents manfully supplied me with all three, and I was momentarily grateful. Ah, but they *added* something. With no signal from me—and perhaps as a slightly unnerved nudge toward manhood—they likewise provided a midget automobile: one of those pint-sized cars that I could climb into and pedal away. It was milk-chocolate brown with a snazzy orange stripe, a deafening horn; and I hated it on sight. No known reason why.

Yet—even at four—I'd managed to learn that I must
instantly bury my disappointment. Neither Mother
nor Father must see a trace of rejection on my face.
There are further photographs from that day to show
that I managed to drive the car round with an excellent imitation of a grin. In fact I seriously doubt they
ever knew how I wanted to *junk* it or, at the least,
deliver it promptly to the nearest orphanage. It was
likely my first real social success—that lightning acqui-
sition of a skill I'd need forever: the skill of taking
from loving hands a gift I neither wanted nor needed.

I came, in time, to enjoy my car and drive it often.
But while I went on dressing in my feathers and telling
Shirley my private woes, when the next winter came,
I managed to offer the car to a boy who lived nearby
in a huge unlucky family. He took it without the least
hesitation; Mother and Father never chided me once,
though they went on posing that same dilemma so
long as they lived; and I went on hiding my complex
consternation. The memory of it still haunts these
short dark days.

1996

SUMMER ON THE DEEP

Summer begins and my friends board jam-packed airplanes for trips to Europe, Asia, Antarctica — all with the ease of a routine stroll. When I finished college, though, four decades ago, I made my first crossing of the North Atlantic on one of the great commercial liners — five unblemished days at sea. You went by liner then for one of two reasons. Either you had the money to sail first-class and enjoy a week of deluxe quarters, food, and entertainment; or you were glad to share a third-class cabin with strangers for a remarkably small cost.

The sixth — and last — ship crossing I made was in May of 1962, and I sailed on the new and elegant SS *France*. It was the only one of my trips for which I was able to splurge on a second-class private cabin. Other times I shared my space with fellow students, aged immigrants from Poland with ghastly war stories and agonizing snores, or fortyish teachers with rapturous dreams of the Britain before them (Shakespeare, Ten-

nyson, Mary Queen of Scots!)—dreams that had them
proclaiming verse in the midst of their sleep. But I
could take them in youthful stride and sleep through
deafening symptoms from the souls of strangers an
arm's length away.

If youth weren't cause enough, the intense idle-
ness of ship life would have conked the worst insom-
niac. Even in third class, meals were enormous. On
the *Queen Mary* and the first *Queen Elizabeth*, breakfast, lunch, teatime, and dinner had the starchy heft of
British cooking at its postwar stodgiest: tons of potatoes,
ten kinds of bread and bread pudding for dessert. In
fact shortly after my first crossing, I developed dire
stomach problems; and after elaborate X rays, I was
informed by my English doctor that I was suffering
from a normal reaction to first contact with his starch-
bound national cookery. French liners were lighter on
the breads, but every dish was prepared with pounds of
sweet butter, an alternate challenge.

So frequent naps were required—an after-breakfast
snooze, an afternoon wine-drugged wallow in one's
narrow bunk, a nine-hour submersion at night. Otherwise life on the great liners differed markedly from that
on present-day cruise ships. For instance the population of liners was widely varied in age—white heads
were occasionally visible; but most of us were young
to middle-aged, and almost all were bound on a serious purpose: graduate study, a Fulbright lectureship,
a mate to join at some NATO air base. And of course
there was always the saturnine Man or (sometimes)

Woman of Mystery who sat in the bar in severe black and was either an insidious provocateur in the Cold War or a hungry seducer fabricating glamour to cadge drinks or a lucrative tumble on the floor of a lifeboat.

What I loved most, though, in liner life was the fact that you could always find your own desolate corner — a sunny deck chair or the plunging bow railing — and for hours on end slowly savor the fact of your utter anonymity, irresponsibility at its purest; the pounding elation of the actual fact that soon you could land in France or England, smile through customs, discard your passport, and start again as a whole new creature. I could call myself, say, Sebastian Rodwell. I could mimic a seasoned Oxford accent and commence the life of a — what? — self-effacing desk clerk at a small hotel on the fierce coast of Cornwall, spying in unbroken beneficence on decades to come of transient couples who'd never think to ask my true name nor meet my eyes.

1997

A STANDING READER

Even if you've been a lifelong teacher of poetry as I have, you seldom spend a casual evening with like-minded friends reading poems. All competent teachers are, after all, convincing actors; but we limit our audiences to the ranks of youth, not our grown colleagues. To burst into recitation at an English Department dinner party would be serious indication of mental decay, or at the very least of runaway self-regard.

All the pleasanter then to report that recently I sat at the exhausted remains of an excellent dinner at the home of two fellow teachers of poetry. The other guests were an academic husband, his painter wife, and the wife's ninety-year-old mother from Wales. The lady had flown straight from Wales to North Carolina only two days earlier but gave no trace of jet lag or the least surrender to age. She'd said little at dinner, though, despite the fact that her musical Celtic voice was welcome.

Then there came a moment over coffee when someone mentioned Keats's age at his death—was he twenty-
five or -six? The awful answer was barely twenty-five; and
then I, emboldened by wine, heard myself reciting the
lines that are often called Keats's last. They're as brief
and crushing as any—

This living hand, now warm and capable
Of earnest grasping, would, if it were cold
And in the icy silence of the tomb,
So haunt thy days and chill thy dreaming nights
That thou wouldst wish thine own heart dry of blood
So in my veins red life might stream again
And thou be conscience-calm'd—see here it is—
I hold it towards you.

Keats's vehemence seized the table; and soon our
hostess had taken down the Norton anthology; and we
were going round the table reading brief favorites—
Thomas Wyatt, Yeats, Stevens, Auden. Our skills varied but I noticed that most of us were watching our
eldest companion as the book made its way toward her.
What poem would she choose? Would her eyes see it
in this dimly lit room?

At last the hefty volume reached her. Wearing no
glasses, she turned to the index, then looked up and
said "The poem I truly remember is 'Hart-Leap Well'
by Wordsworth. It's not in this book."

Our hostess stepped to a shelf, found a complete
Wordsworth, and presented the lady with the actual

poem—some three pages long in minuscule type. Surely she'd never decipher such code.

But she took a silent moment to skim the pages, then stood in place—all the rest of us had read from our chairs. Holding the book out well before her toward the overhead lamp, she told us she'd learned the poem as a schoolgirl. Then she spoke it straight through with barely a falter, a poem much longer than any we younger readers had dared. As she reached the end—

> Never to blend our pleasure or our pride
> With sorrow of the meanest thing that feels—

she looked round herself as though returning from a world that had died long before us.

I've heard more artful recitations but none more uncannily convincing. Not only had she read it against the opposition of her age; but as she sat again, I realized that this smiling woman beside me was born only five decades after Wordsworth's death, a poet as great as any since Milton.

Her name is Ella Williams; and in the bravery of her choice, she offered us a good deal more than she knew—she'd done her sizable best, on foot, to give us that much of a look at the Earth in clearer days, four thousand miles and many light-years from here and now.

1997

A GALLOP DOWN
THE HOMESTRETCH

Since I began writing my first substantial piece of fiction in 1958, I've written in a good many other forms as well—poetry, drama, the essay. Like any particular track or field event, each brand of words has its own rules and makes its own demands on the writer's focus and stamina. I'm often asked if I have a favorite form, a particular event that gives me the most gratifying sense of workout. I answer truly—No. A four-line poem written in a twenty-minute sprint, or the twelve-month marathon of a five-hundred-page novel can feel equally rewarding in the surge and then the wake of its completion.

It would be a lie, though, not to confess that the work on a novel—and the final days of that work—can feel as uniquely invigorating as a month by the purest Norwegian fjord, being splendidly fed as spring climbs toward me with clean sun and flowers. In apprentice days, I experienced my share of the miseries of any job—the uncertainties of skill, failures to understand the importance of physical training and pacing, the slowness of progress. I can remember early nightmares as I reached the final hard fifty pages of a manuscript. In those dreams, I'd enter a bookshop to find that someone had spirited the fretted-over manuscript out of my house and published it without me.

In the past decade, an encounter with cancer has altered my mind and body in ways I don't entirely comprehend. As one of the results, in any case, the process of writing a novel has become one of generally uninterrupted pleasure with a final bonus jolt of elation as the end comes in view. And that elation offers so many of the addictive qualities of other joys—athletic exertion, sex, splendid cooking, participation in intense moments of music or sacred ritual—that I've indulged it as frequently as possible: six times in the past eleven years.

The latest birth is a tall stack of paper called *Roxanna Slade*. It's a first-person story, the life of a woman born in 1900 and alive to tell her story today. The fact that I'm unquestionably a man undertaking her voice has been one of the bigger pleasures of the job, as it's been more than once before in my work. To enter daily, for a long stretch of months, the eyes and mind of a separate creature is lure enough to draw a born writer on through long miles of story— Roxanna, for instance, relates a full ninety-four years of life.

For a man to enter, to such an extent, the mind of
a woman is as powerful a draw, however risky. But
I've braced myself with a single uncontestable fact—
like most men, I was reared almost exclusively by
women. In venturing to cross the gender line—a line
we all exaggerate absurdly—another onward pull
began to take me. As a life took shape (with all its surroundings of parents, mate, children, friends, enemies), I came to think I was attempting at least a steady
bow to the tribe of women—white and black—who
made my childhood a safe and tempting school, a
well-lit room in which I was asked to learn one skill
before all others: unguarded sympathy for the life of
my species and the Earth around us. Whatever *Roxanna Slade* achieves, she's passed through barnacled,
battered me in that first hope and warmed my heart.

1997

PORTABLE MUSIC

If I were king of American education, I'd override states' rights and institute more than one universal requirement for all our young citizens. One requirement would be that, after two years of high school, every student must pause and spend twelve months in useful national nonmilitary service. There'd be other sensible requirements—all students, for instance, would spend serious time in the actual impersonation of cripples and the aged: they'd undergo long periods immobilized in wheelchairs or seated all day in nursing homes to learn what time has in store for us all—if we live so long.

More cheerfully, though, I'd require that everyone learn to play a portable musical instrument—not a toy like the kazoo but something as serious as the flute, the guitar, the mandolin, the Celtic harp and bagpipe, the Indian sitar, the Japanese koto, and dozens of other possibilities—not to forget the human voice. One of the happier aspects of the 1960s and seventies was the prevalence of a guitar and a voice willing to sing in virtually every house, but that pleasantness has evaporated now to be replaced by nothing more helpful in the business of life than the din of canned radio or the soul-frying boom box.

Why a *portable* instrument though? Why not the grand piano, the full-size harp, the cathedral pipe organ? Nothing wrong with those instruments; learn them by all means but not exclusively. Don't make the mistake that I, and so many others, have made. We allowed our hard-earned skills at ponderous instruments to lapse in adult life when we traveled incessantly or lived in places with no piano, say, or church-size organ.

If I'd invested even a third of my youthful hours at the piano in the classical guitar, I'd have today a heart-easing skill. I could sit in desolate airports and hotel rooms, in hospital cells, or alone at home and console myself with a skill that is likewise a sizable gift to other humans. As it is, I sit on airplanes now with my headphones tapping a CD player, hearing Handel or Haydn or James Taylor—which is pleasure surely but nothing compared to what I might make with my own hands, if only my hands knew the secrets of a portable instrument.

While awaiting my benign reign, then, as king of our schools, lure every impressionable child you know toward a source of music that can be transported, at the very most, in no more than two arms.

1997

A MOTTO

No one I know has a motto these days. In my childhood, a personal motto was recommended to me by several of my teachers. My father showed me that his eldest sister had tracked down the family arms — a lion rampant — and found that our motto was *Vive ut vivas!*: Live so you *may* live! I spurned it as old hat and searched awhile longer, then abandoned the quest. Or thought I had.

Like so many abandoned searches, however, it completed itself when I'd all but forgot it. I was twenty-five, about to leave England where I'd spent three happy years in graduate school; and it came from one of my kindest teachers — an Anglo-Irishman named Nevill Coghill. Nevill was a survivor of the old English landed gentry who'd fastened on the Irish centuries ago, and he'd once been seized at a county fair, hustled round a corner, and lined up against a wall by the IRA for immediate execution by a firing squad till someone ran up and said "No, no, that's Mr. Coghill —

Sir Patrick's son; he's not who we're after." In later calmer years, he'd directed Shakespeare in London with John Gielgud, taught me a class in criticism and one in Milton's poetry; and since he'd also taught two early students of extraordinary promise—W. H. Auden and Richard Burton—I was inclined to listen when he talked.

I remember chiefly the story he told me of his mother's last words. When he was younger, he'd hired a little plane to fly him to Ireland to see her on her deathbed. As the time came for his return to give final examinations at Oxford, he went to her room for a last farewell. She seemed asleep, so he kissed her brow and silently made his way to the door. As his hand touched the latch, though, her voice spoke clearly—"Nevill." He turned to see her ancient hand pointing in the air. He stood in place and she said quite urgently "Remember. I only regret my economies." He nodded and left, aware he'd heard an important lesson.

It became at once a lesson that he passed to me, in the way wisdom moves through time from mouth to ear. Ever since that moment, I've said Lady Coghill's words to myself and to many others a thousand times. Why did six words of such plain good sense strike me so deeply? It was not exactly news. My brother and I were the sons of often broke but haplessly generous parents. Yet for forty years now, in all the moments of costly choice—whether to buy this book or painting, whether to risk that chancy love, or to write that curious-feeling novel—I've heard Lady Coghill's piercing advice; and I've never found cause to doubt her in the smallest particular. I've never regretted a splurge in my life, only my stingy-hearted choices at the sun-baked crossroads of money and passion In love and friendship, food and travel, art and commerce, thanks and praise — every harmless pleasure of life, including the free employment of flesh to ease my mind and honor another's — I only regret my economies still.

1997

THE GAZELLE
OF ISRAEL

I'd gone to Israel with a younger friend, we'd
rented a car; and with no officious guides, we stayed
in Jerusalem and took daily jaunts into that narrow
but potent landscape. One night, though, we slept in
Tiberias on the Sea of Galilee and came down the
next day through Nazareth, then up and down hair-
raising Mount Tabor; and in late afternoon were
making our way southeast through the gorgeous vale
of Jezreel—not merely the site of lush farms and
orchards but of numerous ancient routs and victories, and the marching past of such transient armies
as the legions of Ramses the Second and of Alexander the Great.

While afternoon became pale dusk, my friend was
driving; there was no other traffic; we were tired; and
I glanced five hundred yards to my right toward a low

line of purple hills and suddenly wondered if they
were the slopes of Mount Gilboa, the site of King
Saul's final battle against the Philistines – the battle in
which Saul lost not only his Israelite troops but his
dearest son Jonathan and, at sunset, his own life to suicide. Our map confirmed the guess. It was Gilboa, still
unmarred by human occupation.

I told my friend where we were and reached for
the tiny Bible I'd bought the previous day to read
him the chapter from the Second Book of Samuel in
which young David—soon to be Saul's brilliant and
tormented successor—laments the deaths of his old
antagonist and of Prince Jonathan, David's great
friend. The lament is a poem of such intensity that it
has to have been written by David himself and is
therefore some three thousand years old. But no later
song of loss and regret has yet surpassed its keening
power—

Gazelle of Israel slain on the heights
The mighty fallen

Conceal it in Gath and Ashkelon's alleys
Or the daughters of the Philistine rejoice,
Daughters of the vile uncut exult

Hills in Gilboa no dew no rain no harvest fields—
The shield of the mighty grimed with dust
The shield of Saul stained unready

From gore of the slain from warrior fat
The sword of Jonathan turned not back
Sword of Saul returned not hungry

Saul and Jonathan loved and lovely
Unparted in life, in death unparted
Past eagles swift, past lions strong

Daughters of Israel weep for Saul
Who decked you in crimson hung you with gold
The mighty fallen in midst of war

Jonathan slain upright on the heights
I mourn you brother too dear for me
Your love fell on me spring of wonder
Past all women's love and wonder

The mighty fallen
The arms of war

In half an hour we stopped at the tiny bus station in
Bet Shean and ate ice cream. Nobody seemed to be
waiting to leave, not now at least; but the room was full
of local teenagers drinking soda and laughing in perfectly normal fashion—a vehemence that signaled
their readiness to leave this dead rural scene the
moment they were grown. Did they even so much as
know, I wondered, that only some two hundred yards
beyond us—on the walls of old Bet Shean, a city nearly

as old as civilization — the drained corpses of Saul and all his three sons were hung as battle trophies till, late in the night, some Israelites from Jabesh-gilead came, rescued them, and gave them decent burial only three thousand years ago?

1998

THE MEMORY DRENCH:
WORLD WAR II*

When the fiftieth anniversary of the Normandy Invasion was widely covered a few years back, I remember thinking that now we might lay that war to rest as we've laid to rest other disasters as huge as our own Civil War and the long war of extermination against the American Indian. Relatively recent though such bloody trials are, they are now little known of by most of us under the age of fifty. But about the griefs of World War II, I was wrong.

When we and our Allies concluded the war against the Axis powers in the spring and summer of 1945, I was twelve years old. As the son of a father who'd been too old to fight but was riveted daily to news of the fighting, I'd sat with him by the radio since I was six—since Germany's assaults on its neighbors in 1939—and

*Not broadcast.

we'd listened most evenings to the grim broadcasts. I can still see his broad grave face as he weathered accounts of the inch-by-inch slaughters and victories in Europe and the Pacific.

In my innocence of violence, I could only gauge the dreadfulness of our time by the apprehensions and fears that clouded the usual peace of his gray eyes—moments like the sound of Holland's Queen Wilhelmina as she capitulated to Hitler, Franklin Roosevelt's calling for war the day after Pearl Harbor, and the first liberations of the Nazi death camps with their tales of cruelty on a scale to dwarf even an imaginative child's visions of the worst that could happen.

No memory of my father's response to war is more vivid, though, than the rare smile and elated voice with which he woke me on the morning of June 6th 1944 to say that the morning news was reporting how the Allies had just invaded Hitler's stronghold in France and that, soon now, the war could end. Given the unaccustomed glee that transfigured Father's face as he stood there above me, I thought two things that were typical of a boy in those years; and both thoughts were oddly sad.

I knew that my friends and I must give up the war games we'd played every day with scary enthusiasm, and that Father and I would give up our evening radio vigils. I was wrong, in the short run. But so was my father's premature elation. The war had another fourteen months to run, and hundreds of thousands more to kill—including a favorite cousin who'd die of a sniper's bullet through the brain and the citizens of Hiroshima and Nagasaki.

And now perhaps that great convulsion will never end; since, lately, Steven Spielberg's *Saving Private Ryan* comes at us like Nemesis itself. The film has been rightly praised, and I have no further encomia to offer beyond the strongest of all—that this one film may never let our Second World War die.

Despite the power of the battle scenes in *The Birth of a Nation*, in *All Quiet on the Western Front*, *Apocalypse Now*, *Full Metal Jacket*, and *Platoon*, it's Spielberg's unflinching readiness to show the instant-by-instant sheer butchery of modern war that may prove capable of branding on our minds and the minds of generations to come that war is merely the stupidest resort of humankind, not to mention the cruelest and least availing.

Having said that of course, I remind myself of Robert E. Lee's assertion to General Longstreet at the Battle of Fredericksburg: "It is well that war is so terrible; we would grow too fond of it!" Yet there may be some hope in that serene exterminator's choice of the implicitly masculine pronoun. If we men can never stop loving war, can women not try their urgent best to stop us? We are after all, from the start, their natural sons.

1998

FORTY AND COUNTING

I turned sixty-five last February; thus I've lately undergone the trials of that milepost: the arrival of unwanted "senior-type" mail, the occasional omens (in the watches of the night) of helplessness and death, and a blizzard of suggestions that urge my attendance at retirement-planning seminars. As a man who's spent eight months of most years at work—at his own speed and in his own home—on novels, poems, and plays, I've certainly had no sense of wanting to quit. The other four months of each year, I've taught English literature at Duke University; and the teaching continues to reward me.

Lately, I've passed the fortieth anniversary of teaching my first classes at Duke; and now that the university has no compulsory retirement age, I see no reason to think that I won't just teach on as long as I know my name and can roll in to class. A few of my colleagues continue fine teaching at ages well in advance of mine.

All the stranger for me, then, to have gone to my high-
school reunion two years ago and heard a high proportion of my classmates speak beamingly of their
imminent retirement and pending travel plans—their
hopes for endless golf and grandchildren. That reiter-
ated dream was not only strange to me; it was genuinely shocking.

Not many of my family elders lived long enough to
retire—my father died at fifty-four, Mother at sixty—
but in all the thousands of memories I retain from
childhood, I can't recall the sound of a single man or
woman saying that he or she looked forward to quitting
the thing that they'd done most days, that had passed
time for them and won them their living. I don't even
remember any sound of sustained complaint from
them about the hardness of their days. And most of
them had far more strenuous work lives than mine has
been. Of course they'd originated in a world where the
concepts of *vacations* and *unmitigated leisure* were
nonexistent. Even their ideas of Heaven involved
heavy attendance at choir and harp rehearsals.

So here I sit, at a serious advanced age, thinking
wistfully of that Frenchwoman who recently lived past
120 in good cheer. I'm hoping—avidly—for something, if not so outlandish as her luck, at least sustained and conscious. I'm hoping after all to learn a
thing or two that's true for anybody else but me, then
to pass that word on to anybody listening. I don't expect
to find it on the golf course or by gazing at the turtles

in my neighboring pond. Every instinct in me says it comes from my fingers at a Macintosh keyboard anchored in my office.

1998

CROSSING GENDERS

Most male fiction writers write in the first- or third-person voice of an imaginary male; the same goes for women—their central characters tend to be female. But there are stunningly well-achieved examples of cross-gender writing. No novels about women are more convincing than Tolstoy's *Anna Karenina*, Flaubert's *Madame Bovary*, or Thomas Hardy's *Tess of the D'Urbervilles*; and lest one wonder, all three writers were staunchly heterosexual, not drag performers. Female writers have attempted the crossover less often; but Emily Brontë's Heathcliff in *Wuthering Heights*, Anne Tyler's Jeremy in *Celestial Navigation*, and the whole universe of convincing men in Pat Barker's recent World War I trilogy entitle us to hope for further metamorphoses by attentive women.

Why should there be an imbalance in which male writers have succeeded in gender crossing more often than women? No doubt the explanation is complex and would differ for any writer questioned. I've published two novels, called *Kate Vaiden* and *Roxanna Slade*, which are written in the voice of a woman. When reading from either novel in public, I'm invariably asked by women how I managed such a psychic change—men seldom ask. My answer says first that I'm convinced that Americans have mystified the genders to the point of claiming that no man can profoundly understand a woman or vice versa.

That denial is kin to another fashionable mystification—the claim that members of a particular race or ethnic group are sealed off from significant understanding of another group's thoughts and feelings. Plainly, different genders, races, and nationalities have distinguishing tones and convictions. Perhaps they even have hard-wired genetic differences; but if the arts of fiction, drama, and poetry have established anything at all in their long-running careers, it's the fact of the overwhelming similarity of all members of the species *Homo sapiens*. We love and hate, multiply and perish alone in virtually identical ways. Any attempt to deny that fact is an assault on the everywhere visible unity of human emotion, the needs and demands of our bodies and minds.

As to why certain male novelists have managed successful portrayals of female characters while female writers have seldom attempted the gender cross, I'd have to revert to the answer I received in graduate school in the 1950s. One of my great teachers was Lord David Cecil, the biographer and critic. When I asked him why Tolstoy could manage a successful gender change while, say, Virginia Woolf or Iris Murdoch found it so difficult, he replied with the unanswerable lucidity that was his hallmark. He said "Because men are reared by women; so are women."

The assertion remains an unassailable fact. A sensitively wired boy is likely to spend the early years of his life in largely female company; so are sensitive girls. With many American fathers now more engaged with their children than ever before, are we set for a harvest of deeply comprehended male characters in female novels, stories, and films? I surely hope so.

1998

BEING REVIEWED

I published a novel this past summer — *Roxanna Slade* — and it's been well received by readers and critics, so it may be a good time for reflecting on the strange phenomenon of being reviewed. It's been thirty-six years since my first novel appeared; and while it succeeded and is still in print, it also introduced me to one of the more baffling accompaniments of a career in the arts. You work to ready yourself for the trade — whether it's dancing, singing, acting; writing poems, plays, novels; or directing, conducting, producing other artists' works — then, with any luck, you win the chance to move into public and offer your product.

Audiences come or don't come; they clap or boo; you get or don't get your check; you go to the party or your glum single bed in a chain motel; and then the reviews land. If you're a typical professional and persist, you'll soon be called everything from a deathless genius to a blighted cabbage leaf which will surely prove toxic to unsuspecting children. From the start, I've had an ample share of that whole spectrum; and I've yet to complain. In private I may have thrust hot needles through the eyes of a few imaginary reviewer dolls; but never in public — mainly because, early on, I was offered a useful rudder for navigating such whirlpools.

It came from an older friend who happened to be an internationally praised-and-execrated writer himself. When he'd seen the polar array of reactions my first work got, he said "Never forget that, if you do your honest work in public, there'll be people who hate you for exactly the same reasons as other people love you; and you'll never resolve that contradiction."

Once in possession of so much good sense, I provided myself with a second navigation device. In short, I began to realize that novelists, playwrights, dancers, and architects are by no means uniquely cursed with the speedy reactions of critics. Such reactions are a giant fact of life in general. Don't all human beings who conduct their lives in any arena more visible than a hermit's cell likewise get *their* endless reviews, and don't those reviews affect not only our sense of personal worth but also our literal jobs — our ability to communicate them to a buying world?

Don't the parents of most teenaged children, for instance, get reviews of a scalding intensity to match those of any bad or failed or misunderstood accountant, novelist, or painter? It's worth conceding of course that the critics — whether they come from the *New*

York Times or the children's room—may be right: we may be awful in what we do. And our failures may or may not be reparable.

Yet most of us who've worked at revision are likely to find little change in our public's response. We're likely to go on being welcomed or dismissed very much as before. It's dangerous to console ourselves with prior examples of the misunderstood in art or life—Keats or Frank Lloyd Wright or Maria Callas or our once reviled mothers and fathers whom we wish to thank when it's mostly too late—yet is there a truer thought to guide us than my poet friend's claim that we're loved and hated for the very same reasons? Nothing for it then but to bear up and onward. *Excelsior!*

1999

ENGLAND
IN THE FIFTIES

Forty-three years ago this fall, I sailed with a group of other young Americans to England. We were going to study at Oxford University, in a beautiful busy city ninety minutes from London. Very few of us Depression babies had been abroad, but we'd seen countless British movies and heard countless broadcasts from what was called "our most heroic ally." So we surely expected the accents of British speech and gallons of tea; yet none of us could imagine what an alien place we'd chosen to live in for two or three years.

My first night in Merton College confronted me with the start of a barrage of physical differences. My family had never been wealthy, but we'd come to expect a standard of ease that postwar England could not or would not offer. My private college apartment, for instance, consisted of a large living room and a small bedroom with a splendid view of the beauties of Christ Church Meadow. The rooms, however, were in the world's oldest academic quadrangle Mob Quad, Merton. Their walls were six centuries old, two feet thick, endlessly damp; and the only source of heat in the perpetual chill was one tiny electric heater which gave as much warmth as a single flashlight might have. There was, admittedly, a running-water basin in the bedroom; but the nearest toilet was outside and some fifty yards away in a grim lean-to against the soaring chapel.

The baths were some distance off in the opposite direction and consisted solely of deep Victorian tubs, often foul with the previous user's remains and offering no more than two inches of hot water before the tap streamed ice. You quickly learned when the rugby team returned from matches, and you raced to beat their dirt to the tubs. Meals were plentiful but dismally cooked and so reliant on unflavored starch that the college physician informed me a few weeks later that my abdominal cramps were the result of "carbohydrate shock," a complaint he had seen in just-liberated prisoners of war only ten years earlier.

I could continue that spoiled-boy recital, but the thing to recall is that Britain in 1955 had not fully begun to realize the degree to which it had lost the Second World War. Its empire—the largest in human history—was shattered, its economy rocked; its centuries-long run of worldly pride had barely begun to believe the humility it must soon accept. So a middle-class American's experience there in those years had many parallels with, say, the experience of a young North African who might have visited Rome in the fifth century, as the city and its far-flung dependents were beginning their slow deathwatch.

Yet the England of the 1950s had much to teach a patient visitor, and the lessons which have stayed with me were lessons in the graceful — often elegantly witty — acceptance of severe decline, a decline which Americans must no doubt face in time. I hasten to add that, however alien much of Britain proved to be in that demeaning crisis, its inhabitants did not.

Within a month of my arrival, one of my teachers asked if the English were being beastly to me? When I said that *frosty* was the operative word, he said "Always remember — the English don't *mean* to be beastly, they just don't know you're *there*." Soon enough most of the people I met thawed and were far more helpful than their reputation promised — more attentive and loyal in their friendships than those I'd known at home. For instance the grown man, whose duty it was to wake me each morning and clean my rooms, noted that I was washing my own socks. He gently warned me that, since I couldn't dry them sufficiently in the Thames-valley air, I was sure to give myself rheumatism. He'd take them home and get his wife to dry them "proper."

But even that willingness to laugh and help was offered in its own decidedly un-American style — or *styles*: the styles of Britain then, before the homogenizing triumph of American popular culture, were strongly dependent upon the economic class of the person one dealt with, and the class styles ranged from languid to bouncy. Aside from a few put-downs on the order of "You wretched Americans have ruined so-and-so," I recall only kindness and challenge—an extended conversation of civility, intelligence, and depth which surpassed all prior and most subsequent talk I've encountered. Again in the words of my teacher, who happened himself to be an English lord, "They reckoned they'd hold their own in Heaven." These decades later, in my mind at least, they talk with me still in a cool but near-celestial glow.

1999

THE STAGE, YEARS AGO*

One of the forms of torture we elders like to inflict on all our juniors is the flat assurance that life, in any conceivable aspect, was grander in the old days than anything since — the landscape, the climate, the cooking, the athletes, the joys of love, and the opera singers. One of my darker secrets, in fact, is that life has got better for me, by the decade, since I can remember. Not that I repudiate my lengthening past nor deny that certain foods were once done better, certain sights were less polluted by crowds sixty years ago than now. In general, though, I can't imagine asking to be transported back to any early stretch of my life for a real-time rerun. I'll risk the here and now.

But toward the end of every year, I do recall a single string of weeks in another autumn when I underwent one indelibly impressive set of experiences I've never had matched in all the time since. I had just

*Not broadcast.

completed my undergraduate years at Duke and had
gone to Oxford for graduate work. Oxford is only some
thirty-five miles south of Stratford-upon-Avon, Shakespeare's hometown; and in the fall of 1955 Stratford
housed (as it still does) the Shakespeare Memorial
Theatre. England in the fifties had barely recovered,
psychically or economically, from the Second World
War—the old imperial England, in fact, would never
recover—and two of the startling features of that cold
grim era worked splendidly to my advantage: its professional theater was incomparably brilliant, and ticket
prices were laughably small.

Even then there were old gaffers at Oxford who'd
repeat for you their tales of the Victorian glories of Sir
Henry Irving and Ellen Terry in *The Merchant of
Venice*—I knew one ancient who'd seen Sarah Bern-
hardt and Eleonora Duse—but all such denizens
known to me were prone to concede that in John
Gielgud, Laurence Olivier, Michael Redgrave, Ralph
Richardson, Donald Wolfit, Alec Guinness, Richard
Burton, Edith Evans, Margaret Rutherford, and Peggy
Ashcroft the Britain of the 1950s was enduring a golden
age by any time's standard. And in no more than six or
eight weeks that singular autumn, I trekked to Stratford
enough times to see the following plays with the following casts:

—Laurence Olivier and Vivien Leigh in *Macbeth, Twelfth Night,* and *Titus Andronicus*
—John Gielgud and Claire Bloom in *King Lear*

—Christopher Plummer and Edith Evans in *Richard III*.

Meanwhile in Oxford itself I saw Paul Scofield in an uncut *Hamlet*, and in London I saw Margot Fonteyn and Michael Soames dance Ashton's *Cinderella* to Prokofiev's score.

In America since, I've seen supreme work by Julie Harris, Jason Robards, Leontyne Price, and a blessed few other Americans; but no one has yet dimmed the memory of a few fall weeks in which I — twenty-two and fit for amazement — saw Olivier consumed before my eyes by the crawling evil of Macbeth's craven hungers as Vivien Leigh's gorgeously serpentine Lady Macbeth lured him onward, or the dying strength of Gielgud's Lear like a lightning-struck oak, or Fonteyn's impossible strokes on the air with only a set of arms and legs, very like human limbs but entirely incandescent. Among the many gifts they gave, they each fired me hotter to do my own deeds — somehow as useful, however unlikely. May every young lover alive in the sound of these words now have similar luck and never forget it.

1999

ON THE STONE

We've reached a point in American history when death has become almost the last obscenity. Have you noticed how many of us refuse to say "he or she died"? We're far more likely to say "she passed away," as though death were a sterile process of modest preparation, followed by shrink-wrapping, then rapid transit—where? Well, *elsewhere*. In short it's the single thing we're loath to discuss in public. Can there be many citizens left, then, who've chosen their epitaphs? There are a few famous self-composed epitaphs from recent history. The Irish poet William Butler Yeats provided himself with one of the most striking—*Cast a cold eye on life, on death;/ Horseman, pass by*. Striking and mighty chilling. Robert Frost's is a little warmer—"He had a lover's quarrel with the world."

I've written everything from novels to television commercials (I once wrote the text for a Calvin Klein television commercial, a confession I only now make public); but even I have yet to write an epitaph. That's mostly because I discovered my perfect lines years ago, and they're by another writer. They come in a translation of a Latin poem by the poet Horace — the seventh ode from Horace's fourth book of odes — and the translation was made by the English poet A. E. Housman, a man who died when I was three years old.

In addition to writing his own poems, Housman was one of the supreme Latin scholars of the century; and he told a class of his students at Cambridge University that he considered Horace's original poem "the most beautiful in ancient literature." I can add only that Housman's translation of the original — published in his *Collected Poems* — is, for me, one of the most beautiful in modern English. In English the poem has twenty-eight lines, but the pitch to which it rises — and from which it gravely falls away — is reached in two lines. In listening to them, you need to know that the word pronounced *heir* is spelled h-e-i-r. Here they are —

> Feast then thy heart, for what thy heart has had
>> The fingers of no heir will ever hold.

After a near seven decades of life, and the teaching of two generations of college students, I can think of few truths of which I'd rather remind the young — or the old, for that matter. Unless a heart craves blood and cruelty, its owner should feed it lavishly; and the memory of such indulgences (whether they be of love or the

sight of beautiful objects, deep pleasures of the soul or
the senses) will warm the colder days to come.

Feast then thy heart, for what thy heart has had
   The fingers of no heir will ever hold.

I at least will be glad to rest under that much truth.

1999

MY GHOST STORIES

I'm a person inclined to believe in the uncanny. I hope I have the sense to resist tabloid claims of Venusian triplets born to an ex–Miss America or weeping tortillas in the likeness of Christ; but I hold out occasional hopes that we'll be able to prove the reality of telepathic communication, the authenticity of the Shroud of Turin, or the possibility of visits from the benign dead. Despite the hopes, however, I've never experienced an encounter with anything that appeared to represent a vanished friend or loved one; and I certainly haven't longed for any such.

I have, however, known two thoroughly sane adults who saw inexplicable appearances. The first was one of my teachers at Oxford, Professor Nevill Coghill. Late one night during the summer vacation, he was reading alone in his rooms in an empty building in a college surrounded by a nine-foot-high wall; and all its gates were bolted. As he read, Nevill heard footsteps begin to climb his stairs. Slowly they advanced to his

shut door, stopped, waited; then a hand knocked
lightly. Assuming a visit from some faculty colleague,
he called "Come in." The door opened slowly and
there stood an old woman, poorly clothed and clearly
distressed. A courtly man, Nevill stood— "May I help
you?" The old eyes met his pleadingly; then suddenly
the lamps in his room were extinguished. He said
"Just a moment; I'll get some light." No sound from the
old lady; and when Nevill had found a workable lamp,
there was no one in his open doorway. He descended
the stairs rapidly—no one. The night porter at the
gate said No, he'd admitted no one. Twenty years later,
as Nevill told me the story, he could only affirm that
he'd received an uncanny visit—some baffled ghost,
perhaps from his early past but long since forgot.

The second account came from my mother and was
passed on to me by her neighbor a few days after
Mother's sudden death at the age of sixty. For several
years, Mother had known that she had two cerebral
aneurysms—ballooned arteries—which would likely
rupture and kill her; but she'd been proceeding with
a virtually normal life, alone in a sizable house. Then
on a May morning, she walked to her neighbor's and
told her a story. The previous night, while watching
television, she'd fallen asleep on the couch. When
she woke a few hours later, she stood to go to the
downstairs bathroom before climbing to her bed.

As she stood, she noticed that my father was sitting
absolutely as usual in his chair by the couch where
she'd just napped. They didn't speak and she was

already in the bathroom before she realized that my father had died eleven years ago. She wasn't afraid. Calmly she walked back through two rooms to see him again. He was gone. That was the story—no more nor less. But four hours after telling the neighbor, one of Mother's aneurysms burst.

Moments later she was unconscious, and she died in peace that night. My mother was a rational person, entirely unlikely to have seen a ghost; but as I heard her story, I recalled that the phenomenon of a dead loved one returning to fetch us is anciently reported.

There, for what they're worth, are a pair of stories that I manage still to wonder about. They're a small but real part of my conviction that the world is not only strange but stranger than we're capable of knowing.

1999

THE OLD MAN
IN HERE WITH ME

Before long I'll turn sixty-seven. Hardly a milestone birthday—like sixty-five or seventy—but as it rushes toward me, the prospect has given me occasion to recall a peculiar phenomenon I share with many others. The fact is that, however many years most Americans accumulate, they tend to think of themselves always as being one particular age. Hobbled as I am, I deeply believe that I'm somewhere in my late teens—about seventeen. And I've believed it ever since I *was* seventeen, in 1950.

It's not that I search the coming-entertainment pages for 1950s sock hops, not that I long to join the debating team and argue the legitimacy of the new Communist Chinese government, and not that I have the endless energy of an adolescent boy. But I do quite steadily feel both a boy's ravenous curiosity about the external world and the conviction of my profound unpreparedness for what's coming next.

Some mornings when I'm dressing, I even find myself wishing I could wear my old high-school gray coat-sweater or that yellow corduroy vest that riveted all eyes when I first wore it in the eleventh grade. And more often than I'd like my friends to know, I miss the virtually inexhaustible erotic resourcefulness which no one tells us is unique to adolescence and should be memorized, volt by volt, in clear detail for the steeply declining rest of our lives.

But no, if given the magic throttle to throw myself back to age seventeen, I'd refuse the chance. Sixty-seven might not be precisely the age I'd settle upon, but there's no stretch of my past lasting more than three hours I'd want to repeat. All I might ask to change is the moment of shock I undergo every few days when, absorbed in my work, I have to roll into some room to find a pencil, say. If the room contains a mirror (my house has few), I'm likely to glimpse my real present self—snow-haired and overfed—and think "Who the hell is *that* old guy in here with me?" For a microsecond, I don't know myself; I deny the reality of passing time.

Come to think of it, though, I'd resist changing that too. Einstein after all said "Past, present, and future are only illusions, though stubborn ones."

1999

DOLLS
IN A MAN'S LIFE

In case I should want to deny the importance of dolls in my life, there's hard photographic evidence to convict me. They're pictures from my fifth Christmas. In them I'm displaying my favorite gifts from that bleak Depression year—1937—and all three gifts are from my seriously strapped parents. I'm wearing my new Indian suit, a feather headdress, and a fringed imitation buckskin shirt and pants. In one arm I'm holding a toy shotgun; in the other I cradle a Shirley Temple doll—a new and uncanny likeness of the nation's top star, crowned by golden inimitable ringlets. What boy has ever displayed, earlier and more frankly, the complexity of his needs; and what set of parents has ever seemed less dismayed by the gender complexities of such a list or has bellied up more bravely to their then-only-child's fixed nature?

Then I had virtually no contemporary friends.

Maybe that lack saved me from charges of weirdness. But I know that I no longer have my Shirley, though I still have my next doll—Dopey, one of the Seven Dwarfs from Disney's *Snow White* and unmistakably a boy. Except for one ear, chewed off by my dog, Dopey has survived the past sixty-odd years in excellent smiling shape—a little better shape than I. Other dolls I've lost from the early years include a life-sized likeness of Edgar Bergen's famed ventriloquist's dummy Charlie McCarthy and a finely detailed small Superman. I remember craving my cousin Margaret's husband-and-wife Indian dolls, but in childhood I had no other girl doll after Shirley Temple.

In fact I was twenty-one when I acquired my next. Strictly speaking, it wasn't a doll but a hand-sized fragment of an ancient Roman torso of the goddess Venus. She cost me fifty dollars, was nude, beautiful, and redolent of both eros and antiquity; and she's sat near my desk every day since, helping me understand my need to own, touch, and cherish models of things I love in the world. What else *are* dolls? So from my Venus onward then, I slowly acquired the remainder of my set.

There are small heads of Greek boys and girls, of Alexander the Great and Jesus; whole-body images of Japanese sages, sublime though palm-sized. In all the years of collecting these likenesses, I've bought only two that are full life-sized. One is a stone head of the Buddha. The other is a Roman torso of a nude man, no head and arms but bursting with sufficient life to be a god, though he's likely to be some local boy from the local gym. Not many days pass in which I don't manage to touch them all.

Strangest, though, are the *literal* dolls I got some fifteen years ago as I made my way through a longish tunnel of spinal cancer. One is a grinning open-armed boy from the Cabbage Patch line, the other a life-sized baby in flesh-colored plastic. He wears a diaper and has a boy's equipment. The Cabbage Patch boy I requested at Christmas 1984 when a friend asked me, as my legs paralyzed, for a gift suggestion. The plastic boy I mail-ordered directly. To this better day, they lean by the wall at my library door. I've said why I think I got the other copies of humans, maimed or perfect; but why—when I was fifty-one years old, in mortal danger—I acquired two more children's dolls (one smiling, one frowning), I can only guess. Maybe I longed for the care and company of actual, utterly loyal offspring who'd see me through. Maybe they did.

1999

THE GREAT
IMAGINATION HEIST

T he statistics are famous and unnerving. Most high-school graduates have spent more time watching television than they've spent in school. That blight has been overtaking us for fifty years, but it's only in the past two decades that I've begun to notice its greatest damage to us—the death of personal imagination.

In all the millennia before humans began to read, our imaginations were formed from first-hand experiences of the wide external world and especially from the endless flow of stories passed down in cultures founded on face-to-face narrative conversation. Most of those cultures were succeeded by widespread literacy; and the ensuing torrent of printed information, recordings, and films grew large in making our individual imaginations.

Among the blessings of my past, I'm especially grateful for the fact that I was twenty years old before my

parents brought television into our home. Till then, I'd
only glimpsed it in store windows and had never
missed its brand of time-killing. Like millions in my
generation, I was hardly unique in having spent hundreds of childhood hours reading a mountain of books
and seeing one or two movies in a public theater each
week. Like our ancient ancestors, too, I had the big gift
of a family who were steady sources of gripping and
delightful stories told at every encounter.

I, and my lucky contemporaries then, had our imaginations fed by an external world, yet a world of nuance
and suggestion that was intimately related to our early
backgrounds of family and friends. That feeding left us
free to remake those stories in accordance with our
growing secret needs and natures. Only the movies
offered us images and plots that tried to hypnotize
us—to channel our fantasies in one direction only—
but two to four hours of movies per week were hardly
tyrannical.

To say that is not to claim that people who matured
before the triumph of TV possessed imaginations that
were inevitably free, rich, and healthy. It is to claim
that an alarming number of younger Americans have
had the early shoots of a personal fantasy life blighted
by a dictatorial daylong TV exposure. And not merely
blighted—many young Americans have had their
native fantasy life removed and replaced by the imaginations of the producers of American television and
video games.

My gauge for measuring this massive imagination

heist has been my experience with college students in the composition classes I've taught through four decades. When I remove the lenses of nostalgia, I won't claim that the quality of most undergraduate narrative prose in the 1950s was brilliant; but I'm convinced that the imaginations of my present students have suffered badly. When you asked a student of the fifties to write a story, he or she was likely to give you an account that involved personal feeling—a scene from Grandmother's funeral, the death of a pet, the rupture of a marriage, and often family happiness.

Ask the same of students now, and you're likely to get a story that amounts to an airless synopsis of a made-for-TV movie—a stereotypical situation of violence or outlandish adventure that races superficially along, then resolves in emotionless triumph for the student's favorite character. Instead of a human narration, you get a commercially controlled and commercially intended product. *Sit still; buy this.*

How bad is that? Awful—for our public and private safety as well as for most of the arts. What can we do about it? Short of destroying all television sets, computer screens, and video games, I'd suggest at least one countervailing therapy: good reading, vast quantities of active or passive reading—and reading which is, in part, guided by a child's caretakers. No other available resource has such a record of benign influence on maturation. Give every child you cherish good books—human stories—at every conceivable opportunity. If they fail to read them, offer bribes—or whatever other legal means—to help them grow their own imaginations in the slow solitude and silence that makes for general sanity.

1999

JOKE-TELLING
LESSONS

My father died half a century ago. Though both his sons are writers with long particular memories, most of his acts and traits are lost. Among my recollections, though, are the few times when he gave me instructions for important tasks. I can still change a tire as he prescribed, with infinite caution that the jack not collapse. I never leave home for more than a night without unplugging the hazardous appliances and throwing crucial breakers. At the end of each day, I arrange my watch, my pocket change, and personal totems just as he did on the desk. And I catch a ball exactly as he showed me — both eyes riveted on nothing but *ball*.

Yet I hear him most clearly in the moments when I start to tell a joke or any story that wants an audience. Father was a locally much admired wit; his very entrance into a room could trigger smiles. Yet like so many famous raconteurs and comic actors, he was a large and melancholic man. Among his peers, he reminded me only of Jackie Gleason in Gleason's prime. A similar combination of bulk and sadness in a body capable of a dancer's grace was the groundwork that underlay any story Father told, any of his endless imitations of eccentrics or ludicrous fools. He could literally *become* the aged Miss Georgie Lacoste singing a hymn in church and turning all directions to frown on latecomers.

From early childhood, I learned to predict Father's performances as I saw his face undertake a silent change toward the moment when he'd begin his quick act. What I didn't notice then was how urgent to all his successes was the one word *quick*—the mercy of his perfect brevity. Hold your audience to the fullest extent of your skill—regale them, scare them, astound them as you turn into other people before their eyes: people they know or threatening strangers—but do it quickly with no unnecessary gram of speech and gesture. *Be* Dr. Taylor, the wildly odd town dentist who sterilized his tools with nothing more potent than cool tap water and who once broke a rib of my Aunt Mary Eleanor's as he pulled a wisdom tooth, but be him perfectly and quit the act *fast.*

In childhood I can't have understood the word *elegance,* but I understood that my father's aim was the use of his own best faculties to win approval in the happiness of his audience and to earn it through the exercise of plain elegance—the achievement of maximum response with the barest minimum of graceful effort. But from mid-adolescence, I felt compelled toward a similar success. At family gatherings I'd venture to tell my own stories or repeat our tribal memories. And I took encouragement from my kinfolk's smiles; yet I also glimpsed a strain of impatience—I was not my father; where was he? I was, at most, his opening act, all elbows and thumbs. Ignorance, or pride, kept me from asking for help from my main helper.

Luckily it was midway through my sixteenth year— when Father was giving me a driving lesson—that he quietly confided the secret which propelled his success as a jester, a bard, and finally a man. My problem with a stick-shift car was managing the clutch—releasing it steadily, to avoid stalls or lurches. On a day when I'd lurched us badly, Father finally said "*Pull* over here please and stop." When I'd brought us to rest beside a pasture, he turned his gray eyes on me and said "Son, the thing you need in all you do is to do it quicker but also gentler. People, and even this Buick car, won't *wait* for you. Their lives are too short."

Somehow his lesson reached me at last. I can't claim that, since, I've driven my cars and performed my acts with elegant brevity—with Father's wish to ease people's lives through a momentary grace, with his determination not to bore one soul—but I haven't quit trying.

1999

WHAT MY PARENTS
DIDN'T TELL ME

T hough my father was born in 1900 and my
mother in 1905, they came from free-talking families—big mixtures of voluble children—and they
shared an enviable candor. In childhood I never wondered how my kin acquired their freedom from puri-
tanical restraints though now I can guess that it rose
from their confidence in being small-town gentry—no
money but good standing. Further, they bathed in
one of the old South's privileges—a daily compan-
ionship with African Americans who never saw the
realities of the human body as shameful.

Not that my parents overwhelmed me with premature information. They employed an easy decorum when I was present, though I relished the times
when their contemporaries arrived; and decorum
slipped enough to permit the jokes that began to give
me my first hint that delights awaited me when my

body bloomed. But physical delight was by no means the central theme of their talk.

Without preaching, they laid out before me a clear road map toward decency; and they sign-posted the route with rare warnings. One example — when I was twenty, Father was driving me back to college for my fraternity initiation. The group I'd chosen was hardly a temperance society; but as Father let me off, he — who'd conquered his own alcoholism and seen a number of his family lose the fight — offered one sentence only. He said "Darling, remember — the men in your family were never too good around liquor." He never mentioned it again. The warning stuck.

Lately, near that honorable man's hundredth birthday, I've been mulling my parents' gifts and wondering if there were some useful thing they could have told me but didn't? I'm not an inveterate faultfinder, but the question has arisen because I've been talking with friends who have children and are wondering about their instructional duties. The fact that I've had no child makes me an expert on the subject — yes? — so I'll offer only one suggestion beyond the normal hopes that deep courtesy, kindness, and the avoidance of self-absorption be taught as early as possible. My suggestion can be stated briefly — *Teach them hope.*

The great cause of unhappiness in my own lucky childhood was a lack of hope. When something went wrong, I assumed that my unhappiness would last; it would become the prevailing weather of my life. All the children I've known are frequently hopeless, far into adolescence. They're often trapped in secret misery because they lack an assurance that most adults possess—the assurance that, sooner or later, all signals change. Red lights turn green; the cold rain stops. But children have no such confidence. Their sense of the mercy of time is severely limited; why should they trust in any healing power? Hence, not only their sadnesses but their suicides and much of the violence that leaves adults so baffled.

I had only one long grief in my youth. It lasted nearly three years, and I still wonder how I survived it. I also wonder if my parents might have found a way to sit me down and gradually convince me that my grim weather would improve, that the two friends who'd become my tormentors would soon go their own ways—that I'd gain some power in daily life. They knew of my torment. They affirmed that they loved me; but at my self-obsessed age, that was of slim help. How could they have helped me open myself to plain good sense? Few offspring of sane parents are entirely impervious to reasoning.

Was there no way I could have heard my mother and father say, if they'd tried, that the very nature of life is *change*—often change for the better? I don't know what words I'd have put in their mouths; but I'm sure that every parent and friend of the young badly needs that skill.

2000

THE COMMONEST
DEMON

At the start of each semester, when I tell my students how important it is that they attend class regularly and participate in all discussions, I add that—as a veteran of the school and college experience—I'm more than aware of how constantly the demon of depression stands in the shadows of every student room, waiting its moment to strike and smother. All adolescents are especially likely victims—and most college students are teenagers till the end of their sophomore year.

No one gave me a similar warning, when I left home and moved into a dorm; but I well recall that—within weeks—I was far too familiar with the ceiling of my room. I'd memorized its stains and cracks as I lay on my bed and gazed above in fatigue, uncertainty, and the general powerlessness of youth. Yet good luck in my body chemistry and an appetite for books saved me, then, from the lethal currents that lie only a little below such habitual upward gazing.

Even in the calmer 1950s, I watched half a dozen of my friends take to sleeping round the clock, then flunk out, or drag in misery toward a pointless diploma. It was years, though, before I learned that a favorite member of my own family had suffered psychotic depression, with a suicide attempt, in the early years of my childhood and that two family friends had succeeded in killing themselves in the depths of melancholia. Despite those discoveries, still I waited a long while before deciding that I should at least alert my own students to the danger and offer them advice if they felt the need—the advice goes no further than an encouraging suggestion that they visit our university's excellent counseling services.

And I made my decision when I came to see how, increasingly through the 1980s and nineties, somewhere around ten percent of my students were giving at least the early signs of entering emotional deep water—blank faces, frequent absences, lack of involvement in class conversation, and an evident unawareness of the possibility that they were already well into depression: a disease for which, at least, we have generally effective treatment. I've come to think that my own years of denial of the spreading epidemic were grounded in the same comforting blindness that's still so common to parents.

Only recently a student told me that she'd finally informed her mother of the helpful treatment she was receiving for suicidal depression. The mother's reply was to seize her daughter's medicine, pour it down the toilet, and say "Nobody in our family has ever been crazy, and you're not going to start it!" My young friend is alive and stronger still but only because she reminded herself she was now a legal adult and could seek her own care. Among the huge crowd of the troubled, however, hers is far too rare a victory.

2000

WITH IDA

I never really knew my grandmothers—one died before I was born; the other when I was four. So I didn't have a natural choice of love from women older than my mother. I had six aunts, three on each side. Father's sisters were women of wit, independence, and durability. Mother's sisters were more nearly traditional women of their time, lively but finally acquiescent wives and mothers. So it was from Mother's side that I chose a woman to be my refuge from the intensities of those eight years when I was the only child of my financially and emotionally harried parents, loyal though they were.

I chose Aunt Ida. She was eighteen years older than Mother and had reared her when their own mother died. Ida was, then, very nearly my own mother's mother; and she quickly became my working grandmother. As my father's search for late-Depression employment took us to other small Carolina towns, we lived away from the family home in which Ida and her

husband had raised three boys of their own; but since
that house was my mother's birthplace, we returned
there at every conceivable excuse for the food and
talk which were the chief rewards of the Southern
white middle class (and virtually the rest of the nation)
in those years.

Ida had been present at my birth, her own sons
were grown; and even before I could choose to love
her, she apparently chose me. She had a marked pref-
erence for boys, and I was a willing recipient. By the
time I was two, we were fully launched on a mutual
devotion that would see us through the remainder of
her long life. For all my fierce need of my gentle parents, I'd welcome any hour with Ida like a spotless
month on a perfect island.

Extended families in those days were strung, like
immense cat's cradles, on just such cross-generational
transactions; and often they were sanity-saving nets. Neither of my parents showed a sign of jealousy of my bond
with Ida. In fact, when they were ready to leave her
home after a visit, they'd have to wait till I was asleep;
otherwise there'd be much bawling.

Their trust in the bond seems strange, in light of a
reality I learned of years later. In my infancy, Ida was
embroiled in profound psychotic depression — a seizure
that lasted some five years. At one point she spoke to my
mother of her fear of harming her own youngest son,
Ida's son. It was a hell which ended only when an apparent suicide attempt inflicted a grave head injury that
somehow set her right. Yet through all that, my parents

never feared to leave me alone in the care that Ida so obviously longed to give me.

By present standards, their trust in her ability to sustain an entirely benign love for hours—and some-times days seems at the least inadvisable, at worst reckless. Given that Ida was my mother's own foster mother, they perhaps had firm grounds for the trust; but Father was an anxious man, ridden by fears. Did he express no concern to my mother?

They're all long gone now, and there's no one I can ask for further understanding. What remains is the fact that my aunt, a woman in the grip of the cruelest human illness, somehow saw me as an embodiment of hope. And though she lived till I was thirty-three years old, we never mentioned what we'd given one another, though still we could sit alone together and silently feel entirely safe.

2000

A PERFECT DINNER

I t's a tired old party game; but if you could pick,
from all history, one or more persons to dine in your
home or to meet you for dinner, whom would you
pick? In childhood I read, more than once, a book in
which Hendrik Van Loon imagined a series of such
dinners. It set me off on plans of my own. Then, my
ideas ran to figures from the distant past—heroic types
like Alexander the Great, Cleopatra, Charlemagne,
Joan of Arc. It didn't occur to me that we'd be
marooned in our separate cultural backgrounds and
would have virtually nothing to say to one another—
thus there'd have been much silent chewing and, in
some cases, deep drenches of wine (Alexander was
prone to drunken violence at dinner).

Later, in England I attended a small dinner given
by the biographer Lord David Cecil. The poet W. H.
Auden was guest of honor; and it was Auden—a lover
of parlor games—who went round the table, chal-
lenging us to compose a perfect guest list. As we each

produced candidates, Auden at his most pontifical would explain why the name was acceptable or not. I remember suggesting Jane Austen only to have him say "A hopeless mouse at table."

When we'd got round to Auden's own second choice, however (his first was Richard Wagner), he said "Shakespeare of course"; and Lord David rose to the challenge—"Ah, Shakespeare. Now he truly would have been silent. Can there ever have been a more dedicated listener in the history of the human race?" Oddly, I don't recall our final list. It did, though, include Lord Byron and Oscar Wilde—two of the supreme talkers.

Four decades since, I was eating alone the other night, felt a little lonely, and found myself playing the old game. What other person would I most want here? I disqualified all missing friends, loved ones, or kinsmen and limited myself to departed strangers. First, I considered those whom we know to have enjoyed convivial meals—Socrates, Jesus, King Arthur, Dr. Samuel Johnson, Henry James. Each seemed, on reflection, a little overwhelming. I wanted a conversation, not a tidal wave. So my options narrowed quickly. Think of how many supreme conversationalists you've known in your life, as opposed to monologists, and you'll watch your chances dwindle to almost nothing.

I was surprised to be left with Abraham Lincoln, a perhaps unenterprising choice for an American. And indeed if I were out to eavesdrop on dazzling monologues or to watch a stunning beauty at close range,

I'd have hardly chosen Lincoln. But who else would listen so closely and engage me so continuously? I could have told him about something as dull as my latest visit to the dentist and got a funny response. I could have expressed my concern for Mrs. Lincoln's endless personal difficulties and tapped the mysteries of that puzzling marriage.

Finally, I could have pressed him to help me plumb the darkest mysteries of my home and my kin: mysteries that he himself shared from his birth. How were men and women of the decency and compassion of his and my relations enrolled and maintained in a system of racial evil as cruel as any other we know of? To the best of my knowledge, no one pressed Lincoln quite that far in his days on Earth. My guess is that he'd have tried to tell me what I most want to know.

2000

KEEPING AN EYE OUT

I have a small talent for landing near the famous, with no prior plan—especially the famous who're in some form of hiding. Early one Sunday morning when I was twenty, I was staring into Tiffany's window at a confection of diamonds and emeralds when a voice at my ear said *"That* would take you a long way into many boudoirs." It wasn't quite what I had in mind, but the voice had a plummy familiarity—a 1940s radio voice of fine mahogany, rum soaked. I thought I knew its source; and when I turned there indeed was Orson Welles, astoundingly tall and in one of his thinner phases.

He was as unaccompanied as I, and Fifth Avenue was as deserted as it gets. Maybe wrongly, I thought it would be desperately unsophisticated to grin and call his name. I managed a few words of flat-footed agreement with his view of the jewels and went my way. Do I flatter myself, nearly fifty years later, to imagine that he looked a tad forlorn as I went? After all, I'd been told dozens of times that I looked a lot like "the young Orson Welles." If I'd lingered, would we have wound up discussing film theory over eggs Benedict just across the street in the Plaza Palm Court?

A few years later I was more subtly persistent as I came out of Harrod's in London. As I exited into Knightsbridge, Ingrid Bergman entered through the adjacent door. By then I'd gained sufficient command of my opportunities to turn and, in my best imitation of Scotland Yard indifference, to shadow Miss Bergman through a tour of the building. Leather gloves, I recall her buying; a Stilton cheese for ship-ping, and a sensible brown sweater from a bin of sale sweaters.

All that and the whole half-hour chance to watch her lanky body in a plain macintosh and above it that head with the face whose radiance had lit mere white-rag movie screens in Hindustani villages and warmed a zillion souls. She gave me no Wellesean glance, though — no hint of muffins in the famous nearby tea-room — and she left as briskly as she'd entered.

Succeeding years and dozens more sightings. Vivien Leigh on the streets of Oxford in the '50s, Greta Garbo on Lexington Avenue in New York rummaging through bargain raincoats in Alexander's basement (each woman about as disguisable as a snow-white tiger at noon); Ronald Reagan on the deserted streets of Beverly Hills, Christmas Day '64, plainly eager to talk about boots in a shut store window.

The funniest came in Jerusalem of all places in

1983. A friend and I had come down to breakfast, both more than a little groggy, in the King David Hotel. We began to eat in deep mutual silence. Then as my eyes cleared, I noticed at the adjacent table—no more than two yards away—an American family; father, mother, teenaged son, grandmother, and a professional tour guide.

Holy mackerel! The father was unquestionably the great troubadour of the 1960s, arguably the most prolific and original of all our native songwriters. And he looked as grimly forbidding of recognition as I'd always heard he was. Still, here he sat in alarmingly domestic surroundings. To inform my breakfast companion without stir, I took a normal-sized sugar packet from the bowl between us and wrote on the packet the clear words "This is Bob Dylan" followed by an arrow pointing to the great man.

My still groggy friend took the packet from me, stared at it incredulously for ten seconds; then said loudly enough to sway chandeliers throughout the huge room *"This is Bob Dylan?"* Every other diner heard the clarion announcement—I'd gone raving mad. But all the Dylans looked to us calmly, the great man smiled palely, and his young son—there to be bar mitzvahed at the Temple Wall—gave a slight shy wave.

A welcome grace on the heels of deep embarrassment. I'm far more private with my recognitions now.

2000

THE SINGLE CORPS

I've never married, never fathered a child; yet I've never been conscious that those omissions have left me maimed. So now—as crowded and waste-poisoned America is lulled by rote affirmations that the nuclear family is the soul of all virtue and hope— I pause to wonder how many others have noticed that the mother-father-child family is likewise the source of virtually all the physical abuse and psychic mayhem which children experience. Likewise, despite the decline in Freudian thinking, it's apparent to any observer that a high proportion of the mental and spiritual problems of all adults spring from the same old family hothouse that drove the Oedipuses and the Macbeths to violence, not to mention the miseries of our own most famous political clan.

For whatever reasons, some ten percent of Americans choose not to marry; at the least, they find themselves unmarried somehow. Ten percent of the population is twenty-eight million human beings—the

population of a respectable middle-sized country. Yet
where are the audible advocates of those who—for
whatever reason—make the far-from-exotic choice
not to marry or cohabit? I've often praised the splen-
dor of those spinsters and bachelors—heterosexual,
homosexual, asexual, or none-of-your-business otherwise—who used to occupy the majority of teaching
desks in our schools and who, in lucky towns, still do.
That a small few of those teachers may have been a
danger to their students hardly demeans the record of
thousands of others as steady providers of services of
the highest value. It may need remarking, conversely,
that the higher proportion of all our felons are married
or will be.

With no desire to court the label of harmless nut or
public menace, I can still wish aloud that a few of our
creditable and fulfilled unmarried citizens—from all
strands of life—would stand to the fore and make
themselves heard, not as advocates for celibacy or any
other purely sexual choice but for chosen *singleness*,
an honorable estate established by God (as the Christian marriage service says of marriage, and nowhere in
the Bible does God deplore it) and rich with the precious gifts of uncrowded time and quiet air that have
given us, age by age, such friends of the human enter-
prise as the scientist-philosophers Isaac Newton and
Ludwig Wittgenstein, the composers Handel and
Beethoven, the poets Emily Dickinson and W. H.
Auden, the caregivers Florence Nightingale and Jane
Hull, the novelists E. M. Forster and Flannery O'Con-

nor, not to mention the thousands of dedicated servants of whatever gender from church or state.

To ignore their presence, their immense contributions, or to eye them askance as an automatically suspect minority—as many touters of family values do daily—is to deny a huge sum of capital in our reach, capital meant for our nation and for every soul among us. The choice, or the accident, of their singleness is not necessarily a whit more difficult than that of the legally joined. It does sometimes mean, though, that the nation's great roosting jamborees—Christmas, Labor Day, Thanksgiving—can find them a little marooned in silence. Whatever you do, don't send the children round with fireworks but think of what one single person, somewhere in your past, has done for you and act accordingly.

Or to be more personal about it (not broadcast)—

The longer I live, the more reasons I seem to discover for the much-befriended solitude in which I've chosen to live since I departed my parents' home for college. A few of those reasons are private, though not outlandish; suffice it that for thirty-three years, I lived alone (with dozens of friends in fairly easy reach). Owing to the uninvited but permanent paralysis of my legs when I was fifty-one, my solitude has been relative for more than a decade. To help me in my wheelchair, an assistant occupies the far end of my house; and I take considerable pleasure in our daily meetings, but many of my Lone Ranger routines continue unaltered. For eight months of the year, I still go to my computer at nine each morning and work a full day in a silent house — on the writing of a novel or poems, an essay or a play.

Like most other workers, I award myself breaks— I make coffee, listen to the news, phone friends, or talk with my assistant as he passes. But for anywhere from six to nine hours, six days per week, I'm absorbed in unaccompanied writing. And while I can scribble on the back of an envelope in a mobbed airport, something deep in my metabolism requires solo days for reliable production. From at least the age of five, for reasons unknown, I crave that solitude, as deer crave salt licks; and I'm far from alone in my need. Does that make me and my lone colleagues self-absorbed narcissists, sterile drones? Far from it, in many cases.

What I in particular go on making from solitude — aside from enduring friendships — are a pair of performances: the first is my work as a teacher of college students for thirty-nine years; the second has resulted in my twenty-eight published volumes of fiction, poetry, essays, and plays. The world will thresh my performances and determine their yield. I can only judge them as what they've amounted to for *me*. They're my literal descendants, and I try to make them broadly useful to a great many others. The several thousand students to whom I've taught reading and writing will either discard, or enact in their own lives, whatever I offered them in their youth. But do I, in Brady-Bunch-

nostalgic America, need pardon for asking how many
blood-parents have the sense of reward that I feel? —
not self-satisfaction but a quiet pleasure that this much
lies behind me and many other lone wolves on a trail
that's by no means as unyielding as the sight of the arid
moon through trees?

2000

ELOQUENT LETTERS

$\mathbf{A}$nyone who reads volumes of letters written by Americans in the eighteenth, nineteenth, and early twentieth centuries may well wonder what catastrophe intervened between then and now when so few of us write letters at all, much less messages of such vivid ease and eloquence as our ancestors produced. A collection like *The Children of Pride*, which gathers the mountain of letters written by members of a Georgia family at the time of the Civil War, will show how visually acute many Americans were in the last century and how capable of communicating their findings to absent friends in unpretentious but memorable letters.

There are hundreds of other collections, from our past, in which we can read letters of a similar narrative fascination and an intensely emotional poetry. Books of letters from any American war make especially powerful impressions of grace in the presence of all but unbearable tension. Given a modest degree of literacy

on the part of the writer, the power of old letters seems
to have borne little relation to the writer's amount of
formal education. Through bizarre phonetic spelling
and broke-backed grammar, still the voices speak out
with the clarity and freshness of a friend in a room —
that welcome and demanding.

What happened that brought us to our present situation in which so few of us exchange letters that take
any degree of care to be entertaining, helpful, and
true to our private concerns? The obvious, though by
no means complete, answer is "The telephone happened." The phone has cast a blight, not so much on
letter writing as on the far older expectation that our
simplest longing for company or our deepest probing
of emotion was expected to emerge onto handwritten
pages that we'd seal and mail off to unseen loved ones,
friends, or enemies.

That human expectation — as old as the ancient
but astonishingly fresh letters unearthed in the Middle
East and Egypt — was not only assaulted by the telephone, it was all but finished by the harrowing clamor
of contemporary life. Who among us can take the
time to sit down each morning, as the earnest well-
heeled Victorians did, and respond to the mail (every
word of it) at unhurried ease? Most of us make a few
urgent phone calls, then lay the balance of the letters
aside with a futile hope to deal with them soon.

What's been lost is not only a revealing layer of
human expression, a stratum of our domestic history,
but also an irreplaceable means of direct but formal

encounter with our associates. Our grandparents were
free to say a great many things in letters that you and
I won't risk saying face-to-face or on the phone. A letter, even back when the post office functioned well,
could take awhile to reach its recipient; and the sender
was spared the sight of the recipient's tears or anger at
some difficult truth the sender might have felt compelled to articulate. A great deal less important business can be transacted by phone than by letter.

Will the new but increasingly omnipresent e-mail
provide us with a chance to recover lost ground? There
is, after all, a valiant—though aging—band of survivors to build on: the men and women who have
never quite let the letter die in their hands. Take a paragraph that came to me a few years ago from one of my
teachers in my grade-school years. "When I was seven
. . . I was alone in a room at Mrs. Herrin's house in
Newberne, Alabama, just trying to read something
and found to my utter amazement that the whole
room had turned around. The desk was on the opposite side of the room and organ, chairs, sofa—everything backwards. I started to the back porch but found
it to be the living room. I had been always alone with
only grown people and I was delighted to tour the
house all strange and north being south. Then rain-
bows came in my eyes and that was more magic."

She's describing the onset of a lifetime of migraine
headaches, a condition that caused her excruciating
pain; but what a gift she makes of so ominous a start-
ing moment—a disease that brings weird blessings

with it. The words, on the paper, are still here in my hand, though my great teacher left awhile back, at nearly a hundred.

2000

A PREMATURE
FAREWELL

Fourteen years ago I was — for the first, and still only, time — borne down the steps of my house by two ambulance attendants. I couldn't walk, I was in pain so hot my head couldn't rise, and I strongly suspected what proved to be true — that a cancer had recurred near the base of my skull. It pressed my brain so hard that I could literally not understand my own voice. I'd speak words that others could hear as normal sense, but to me they sounded like total gibberish — the tongues of rustling demons.

It was a morning in early March, cold though bright; and as the stretcher tilted for the descent, I caught a glimpse of my carpenter friends at work on the east end — new wheelchair-accessible quarters for me in a house that, till then, had been the usual nightmare of obstacles and drops. The addition had some weeks to go; it was costing a hill of money; and at that moment—strapped to a stretcher in the hands of strangers—what seemed undeniable reality poured in: I'd be dead before the carpenters finished. I almost laughed. Three sane young builders were knocking together a handsome shelter for a virtual corpse who was outward bound.

Through the two prior years of crisis I'd generally managed the hope that I'd survive; so I hadn't allowed myself to think of what I'd be leaving if I died. Now, quickly, I thought. I'd be departing, early, a life I'd loved and a beautiful world. Behind the carpenters lay the pond that had seemed a planet in itself—fish, frogs, snakes, turtles, wild ducks and turkeys, a great blue heron, foxes, raccoons, a herd of deer, dogwood and redbud, high copper beeches, and adjacent benign human neighbors.

But earning my nickname, "The Great Indoorsman," I'd watched that planet mainly through glass, the windows that opened from my house on all sides— the pond, the pasture with cattle and horses, the road built more than two centuries ago by a British governor rushing to break a local rebellion. And what I remember thinking next, as the ambulance moved, was two plain things. First, I silently told myself "You've left all that; it's gone for good." Then with no disgust I thought "Good riddance" and felt as stripped of earthly cares as a Buddhist monk in his final breath. Everything I'd gathered and prized—furniture, pictures, the billion memories—was gone. I was glad.

Yet I survived. Fourteen years later, I feel much

like the same man at least. The house seems healthy; its contents have grown and still delight me. But I doubt that they—and all my surroundings—know how I learned (in a wrongly hopeless moment), and have never mislaid, a true secret of inestimable worth: I can leave for good, with considerable ease, when that day dawns, which I hope is not soon.

2000

Reynolds Price was born in Macon, North Carolina in 1933. Educated at Duke University and Merton College, Oxford, he has taught at Duke since 1958 and is James B. Duke Professor of English. His first novel, *A Long and Happy Life*, was published in 1962; and since, he has published thirty-two more volumes of fiction, poetry, drama, essays, and translations. He is a member of the American Academy of Arts and Letters, and his work has been translated into sixteen languages.

Printed in the United States
By Bookmasters